Have Your Promised Breakthrough

Understanding Giving,

Applying Fasting, and Receiving Healing

by Sarah Scarrow

Scripture taken from the NEW AMERICAN STANDARD BIBLE®, Copyright © 1960,1962,1963,1968,1971,1972,1973,1975,1977,1995 by The Lockman Foundation. Used by permission.

Scripture quotations marked (NLT) are taken from the Holy Bible, New Living Translation, copyright © 1996, 2004, 2007 by Tyndale House Foundation. Used by permission of Tyndale House Publishers, Inc., Carol Stream, Illinois 60188. All rights reserved.

THE HOLY BIBLE, NEW INTERNATIONAL VERSION®, NIV® Copyright © 1973, 1978, 1984, 2011 by Biblica, Inc.™ Used by permission. All rights reserved worldwide.

Produced by:

FriesenPress

Suite 300 – 852 Fort Street
Victoria, BC, Canada V8W 1H8

www.friesenpress.com

Distributed to the trade by The Ingram Book Company

TABLE OF CONTENTS

DEDICATION

I dedicate my whole life and this book to the Lord Jesus Christ. Faithful is not a strong enough word to describe who He is! I want the world to know how thankful I am to my Saviour Jesus.

I also want to dedicate this book to my precious three children. Let us continue to stand with each other in love and unity as a testimony of the Lord's grace and goodness. I love you more than I know how to say. You mean so much to me and then some!! Thank you for believing in me. To Matthew, I praise God that the next 15 years will be different than the first 15.

To my mother, Pauline. You are an immense gift from Heaven. God knew what He was doing putting us together as family. Love you so very much.

To my sister, Carla. I so enjoy the times we get to hang out. You are a delight and treasure to me.

To all my dear, encouraging friends. I am truly blessed to know the love and support of people like you. I thank God for you all daily. To Debra George. Thank you, my friend, for writing the forward. Love you and believe for some excellent fellowship together soon!

Sarah

FOREWORD

Sarah Scarrow's "Have Your Promised Breakthrough" is a masterpiece. We all need a breakthrough at some time in an area of our lives. Sarah tells us how to receive our breakthrough and move into the very Best that God Almighty has planned for each of us. I love how Sarah gives her readers the tools on exactly how to apply God's Word and what actions to take to step into His great abundance for your life. Sarah is an amazing woman, mother and friend. I highly recommend this book for all ages and all walks of life. Her writings and teachings will truly enable you to step into your God given purpose and destiny!

Debra George

DebraGeorge Ministries

INTRODUCTION

In this book EXPECT YOUR PROMISED BREAK-THROUGH I share many scriptures. The Bible is a book that was written under the instruction and power of the Holy Spirit. Therefore, it is a spiritual book and we need to invite the Holy Spirit (the Author) to speak to us as we read it. My prayer is that you receive some heavy revelations by the Holy Spirit as you read each scripture and every page.

There is such freedom once giving and fasting and healing is even begun to be understood, that it is easy to understand why the Devil would want it misunderstood and underutilized.

The questions I have contemplated and wrestled with in the past regarding tithing, fasting, and healing are brought up and addressed in this book. I almost want to refer to this book as a manual! If we know how to rightly divide the Word regarding these three vital topic, we will have such a mighty arsenal to go forth with!

Read. Enjoy. Meditate. Rejoice with expectancy for your promised breakthrough.

CHAPTER 1: MONEY WITH A PURPOSE

Finances affect every area of our life, so let's dive into the Word of God to revive revelation knowledge and freedom in the area of finances. We should not just read the Bible for information, but for revelation.

People have often approached me and asked me to pray that they would have a breakthrough in the area of their finances. I have been honoured to pray for many, but you must know that everyone I lay hands on is not made instantly rich! If I did lay on hands and you became suddenly rich, without some teaching from the Bible around your responsibility once you have money, you'd be broke again by next month. I pray that people would hear and obey God in the area of finances and that any blockages to their breakthrough would be revealed. There are many promises in the Bible regarding finances that we will discuss in this book. The emphasis will be on the conditional promises that will not come to pass unless you also do your part. Read each promise in the Bible and see if it hinges on your obedience to do something as a step of faith.

I am all too aware that the word "rich" can cause some Christians to get upset. Rich is not a swear word. The gospel is free, but getting it to the four corners of the earth takes money. The sole purpose of writing this book which includes a section on finances, is so that God's people would be blessed to be a blessing! May you use all your resources (including money) to get the waiting harvest of souls saved. So let us get started digging into scripture regarding giving!

People need teaching on God's economic system (the spiritual laws concerning money). The Bible says God's people (which means born again believers) are destroyed for lack of knowledge. Hosea 4:6: clearly states that God's people are not destroyed because of a lack of power, or lack of ability but because they didn't have knowledge (of the principles). Brothers and sisters in Christ are destroyed for lack of revelation knowledge. If you don't have revelation knowledge concerning kingdom finances, then you are missing out on all that God has for you.

God does not get glory when His children live broke, busted and in lack. If that were the case, then all those people who had house foreclosures or heat turned off or are living under a bridge would be His best evangelists. God is equally not glorified when His people are greedy and consumed with material things. He does not mind us having a home or decent things as long as that is not where our heart is.

"For where your treasure is, there your heart will be also" Matthew 6:21 New American Standard Bible.

There is not one thing that I own that I could not give away. I have things, things do not have me. God is welcome to anything that He has made me steward over. There is not one thing that I own that I could not give away under the leading of the Lord. My desire is to be quick to obey.

I am saddened when people explain to me how they are content as long as their bills are paid, even if they are just barely getting by. In a time when people have lost jobs, I understand the heart of thankfulness for bills being paid, please do not misunderstand that. I am in no way diminishing the precious grace of God who has empowered us to make our mortgage payment every month. Being content and thankful is very Biblical! However, my aim every month is not only to have enough to cover my bills. My desire it to support pastors, evangelists, apostles, teachers and prophets. Do you think that it is somehow beautiful and spiritual to be in lack and not have enough finances to support local and international missionaries? I happen to see that as quite a selfish attitude because you should want enough to take care of yourself plus be a blessing to others. I am long past just wanting my own bills to be taken care of. I am targeting higher goals. There are missionaries (even missionaries in North America) that need your financial support. There are churches that need their mortgages paid off. We all should be going after more than enough money so that evangelists, pastors, teachers, apostles, and prophets are taken care of! There are preachers and evangelists that should not have to be using up time and energy wondering how they are going to make their house payment. There are many ministers that should be in full-time ministry so they can full out focus on souls with all their energy. However, several have to work two jobs (one being ministry) to support themselves because the Church is not taking care of them! I believe in work and do work hard. Currently I am working a "regular" job to pay the bills so this book is taking twice as long to get done as it could if I was able to focus on it full time. Pastors who have to take regular jobs are often leaving their sheep with sometimes not even bare minimum care. There is indeed a ready harvest, but the workers are few. Perhaps that is partly because after our workweek we do not have a lot of energy left over.

> *"Therefore said He unto them, The harvest truly*
> *is great, but the labourers are few: pray ye there-*
> *fore the Lord of the harvest, that He would send*

forth labourers into His harvest". Luke 10:2 King James Version.

Laugh or smile your way up to the front of the church to put your offering in the next time you are in a church service. God loves (takes great delight in) a cheerful giver.

> *"But this I say, He which soweth sparingly shall real also sparingly; and he which soweth bountifully shall reap also bountifully. Every man according as he purposeth in his heart, so let him give; not grudgingly, or of necessity: for God loveth a cheerful giver." 2 Corinthians 9: 6,7 King James Version*

Here are those verses in the New Living Translation:

> *"Remember this - a farmer who plants only a few seeds will get a small crop. But the one who plants generously will get a generous crop. You must each decide in your heart how much to give. And don't give reluctantly or in response to pressure. "For God loves a person who gives cheerfully." New Living Translation.*

How many believers have felt that God is obligated to give seed to every Christian? God supplies seed to only one group of people and that is to the sower. Neither your need, nor your tears move God. Preachers must teach people to sow seed so they will never be out of seed.

> *"Now He that ministereth seed to the sower both minister bread for your food, and multiply your seed sown, and increase the fruits of your righteousness" 2 Corinthians 9:10 King James Version*

He gives seed for food. That means He provides money or provision for you to consume. The verse also talks about sowing (giving) some of your provision. Don't eat what you need to sow as sowing is so that you can also eat tomorrow.

CHAPTER 2: A POOR PERSON GIVING AN OFFERING

The wife of a man from the company of the prophets cried out to Elisha, "Your servant my husband is dead, and you know that he revered the LORD. But now his creditor is coming to take my two boys as his slaves."

Elisha replied to her, "How can I help you? Tell me, what do you have in your house?"

"Your servant has nothing there at all," she said, "except a little oil."

Elisha said, "Go around and ask all your neighbours for empty jars. Don't ask for just a few. Then go inside and shut the door behind you and your sons. Pour oil into all the jars, and as each is filled, put it to one side."

She left him and afterward shut the door behind her and her sons. They brought the jars to her and she kept pouring. When all the jars were full, she said to her son, "Bring me another one." But he replied, "There is not a jar left." Then the oil

*stopped flowing. New International Version 2 Kings
4:1 -5*

What do you have in your house that you can offer to God (to the man or woman of God)? In 2 Kings 4:4 the woman is instructed to shut the door behind her. You do not want any friends with unbelief coming in, looking in, or talking you out of your miracle in any way. On more than one occasion Jesus shut unbelieving people out of the home where a miracle was about to happen.

When there were no jars left, the oil stopped. If she had managed to borrow more jars, perhaps she would have still be pouring oil for a little bit longer. The widow woman's miracle hinged on her being obedient and taking action. She didn't just ask the man of God to only pray for her, but she had put feet to her faith. She had to take action. Faith had to have works with it.

> *"How foolish! Can't you see that faith without good deeds is useless?" James 2:20 New Living Translation*

She had to obey the instruction to go borrow jars from neighbours. Before she saw the increase of oil in the natural, she had to believe it in her spirit and go borrow the jars (and not just a few!) If she would have said, "Show me the miracle and then I'll go talk to my neighbours," nothing would have happened. Quit looking to people to fix everything for you and find out what God's instructions for you are. There is something in your house that you can offer to God as seed so He can meet your need.

This is to preachers and ministers: If you would never receive an offering from a poor person then you are going to leave them poor. There are a few people that have sown into my ministry that did not have a lot of money at the time they gave some. I am positive they are going to get a return on their money if they have not received it already! That's a Biblical concept for all you Bible scholars. It's called harvest. I did not obligate God to bless the people who are givers. *God has obligated Himself to make sure a sower (a giver) always has seed.* I knew some of their financial situations and my flesh wanted to say "No, that's ok. You need to hold onto your money." But the Spirit of God spoke to my spirit this word: "They are sowing into good soil. It is going to spring up 30, 60, or 100 fold. They need a harvest. Receive offering from them so I can give them a financial harvest."

I have proof that it is okay for a man or woman of God to receive an offering from a poor person. I didn't like the idea of receiving an offering from someone that did not have much until the Lord showed me in the Word that it is His way of getting money to people. God is not trying to get money from you when you give. He is trying to get a harvest to you. Some pre-Christians (because unsaved need to get saved, I speak like it can happen) think that preachers are just greedy manipulators trying to take money from people. Sure, there are a few people who have wrong motives and mistreat God's people. You do not have to go use scissors and cut out of your Bible any scripture on giving just because of a few people misusing tithes and offerings. The devil knows how powerful sowing and reaping is. That is why he keeps trying to get believers not to do it. If Satan can get you offended and holding onto your money because of the one percent of preachers that are heretics, then he has successfully blocked a lot of your blessing. If he has a lot of your blessing blocked, then preachers have to go out and work other jobs because you can't support them. It then takes a lot longer before everyone has heard the gospel and the return of Jesus is delayed which suits Satan just fine.

"And the word of the Lord came unto him, saying,

Arise, get thee to Zarephath, which belongeth to Zidon, and dwell there: behold, I have commanded a widow woman there to sustain thee.

So he arose and went to Zarephath. And when he came to the gate of the city, behold, the widow woman was there gathering of sticks: and he called to her, and said, Fetch me, I pray thee, a little water in a vessel, that I may drink.

And as she was going to fetch it, he called to her, and said, Bring me, I pray thee, a morsel of bread in thine hand.

And she said, As the Lord thy God liveth, I have not a cake, but an handful of meal in a barrel, and a little oil in a cruse: and, behold, I am gathering two sticks, that I may go in and dress it for me and my son, that we may eat it, and die.

And Elijah said unto her, Fear not; go and do as thou hast said: but make me thereof a little cake first, and bring it unto me, and after make for thee and for thy son.

For thus saith the Lord God of Israel, The barrel of meal shall not waste, neither shall the cruse of oil fail, until the day that the Lord sendeth rain upon the earth" 1 Kings 17: 8-14 King James Version.

Remember, it is the Lord that sent Elijah to this woman's house! The Lord told him to go to a poor person's house and not to a rich person. To make it even more contrary to what our natural thinking would be, this poor widow also had a child to feed! Elijah had to go and ask her for her last bit of food. How many preacher's would obey that word from the Lord? That would have made headlines today: *"Preacher Asks For Poor Lady's Last Bit of Food."* Haters of Christianity would have a field day with that! Religious people would be all over that! If a preacher would receive an offering from a poor widow today, some people may even go so far as to say that "God would never ask a preacher to receive an offering from a poor person. That prophet is not of God. He is greedy."

If we were in the position of that poor widow, many of us may have been tempted to exclaim to the man or woman of God asking us to give;

> *"I am getting ready to die here and you are asking me to give? I need to receive a miracle right now"*

The Lord didn't send Elijah to a rich person. This widow had a little drop of food left for herself and her son. She figured they would eat it and then sit down and wait to die of starvation. The man of God was sent to her so she could plant seed because she really, really needed a harvest! This was God's way to get a miracle to her. Here is another account in the Word of God to examine:

> *"And Jesus sat over against the treasury, and beheld how the people cast money into the treasury: and many that were rich cast in much.*
>
> *And there came a certain poor widow, and she threw in two mites, which make a farthing.*
>
> *And He called unto Him his disciples, and saith unto them, Verily I say unto you, That this poor widow hath cast more in, than all they which have cast into the treasury." Mark 12:41-43 King James Version:*

Jesus never yelled out "No! That poor woman never should have put anything into the treasury." He never once taught that poor people can not afford to give. He didn't stop her. The son of God noticed that she gave sacrificially as He stood by the offering basket watching everyone's giving. Heaven sees and takes note of your giving. Giving brings us a harvest and we are clearly taught in the Word that we can not afford not to give.

> *"You will be enriched in every way so that you can be generous on every occasion, and through us your generosity will result in thanksgiving to God." 2 Corinthians 9:11 New International Version*

The scripture that tells us that God's plan and will for you is to be blessed enough so that you can be a blessing on every occasion. That verse connects blessing with giving (being a blessing). How many of us are that open with the Lord with our resources? Have you given on every occasion that the Lord has told you to give? You can prove to God that you can be trusted with money by being quick to obey Him. He can be trusted and would not prompt or instruct you to give if He didn't have a harvest waiting upon your obedience.

Money has never been the root of all evil. That is not what the Bible says. Scripture tells us that the love of money is what is not right. Loving anything more than God is evil. It is not what you have that is evil, it's what you love more than Him that is idolatry. Having things is not wrong. Things having you is wrong.

CHAPTER 3: THE TEN
DOLLARS IN YOUR POCKET

People are caught up in the mind-set where they think "If I had a million dollars, I would tithe off of it. I would give God the tithe if I had a million dollars. That is when I would start tithing and giving offerings."

Start with the hundred dollars that you do have! What are you doing with what you have now? What are you doing with the ten dollars that is in your wallet now? Tithe on what you have now. Start there and work your way up with to the million. God says to be faithful with what you have now before you will be trusted with much. Prove to Him that you can be trusted with money.

> *He that is faithful in that which is least is faithful also in much: and he that is unjust in the least is unjust also in much. Luke 16:10 King James Version*

I heard a preacher tell God how much he want to give to missions in the upcoming year, and then left it up to God to determine how much he was going to bring in for income. That is certainly a revelatory way of thinking! Go before God and talk to Him about how much you want to give to evangelists that are getting souls saved. Take steps towards being that type of giver and see what steps God takes towards you. If He can trust you with money, He will want to give you more. He knows that you will funnel it right back into the Kingdom. You have to do the right thing with the ten dollars in your pocket now before you get the thousands. Then you have to do the right thing with the thousands before you get the hundred-thousands.

Rejoice when someone is blessed. There is absolutely no reason to be jealous. Relax! Realize that you are under the same spiritual law as that blessed person. You can put these spiritual laws to work for yourself also. You serve the same God. The devil wants to keep you blinded to God's abundance. When God's people get a hold of this, they start to give to advance the kingdom and that scares the devil. The devil knows that the more prosperity you have, the more you can give to the kingdom. Therefore, he strategizes for you to live below your rights and desires that you perish because of a lack of knowledge. Don't fall for Satan's strategies.

It is an obvious fact that broke people can not help broke people. When I was driving to a near by city to do share Jesus with prostitutes and tell them about the love of God, I needed a car and gasoline. Someone who has no money is unable to financially support what I was doing.

> "Will a man rob God? Yet ye have robbed me. But
> ye say, Wherein have we robbed thee? In tithes and
> offerings." Malachi 3:8 King James Version

I realized that until my tithing reaches 10% I am a thief! A robber is also called a thief. Until my tithing reaches 10% the plain truth is that I am a robber. As long as I am a giver, then I will have seed to give. All I have to do is keep tithing and not robbing God and He will open the windows of Heaven. If you do not tithe and give offerings, it is only your income you are affecting, not mine. God will find a way to keep me going. My income would be just fine because of the harvest I get off the seed that I have planted.

God loves thieves and want them free, but no where in the Bible does it say that He is obligated to give seed to dishonest people. His love is unconditional, but His promises are not. His promises are connected to principles. He doesn't endorse disobedience.

> *"A good man leaves an inheritance to his children's children, And the wealth of the sinner is stored up for the righteous." Proverbs 13:22 New American Standard Bible*

There are men that can not leave an inheritance big enough for their children, so how can they leave an inheritance for their grandchildren also? Many men, if they left earth today, would leave debt to their children and nothing to their grandchildren. That is not what God wants. It is not the will of God for you or your family. Some think this is referring only to an inheritance of godliness and righteousness. It actually is an inheritance of finances because the second part of the verse states, *"the wealth of the wicked is laid up for the righteous."* The wealth of the wicked could never be godliness. The inheritance you are to leave for your children does refer to finances in this particular verse. I do not want to leave my house mortgage to my children or grandchildren.

In Sunday School the teachers often tell us the account of the Good Samaritan and how we are to also be like this good Samaritan. Here is the account in Luke :

> *In reply Jesus said: "A man was going down from Jerusalem to Jericho, when he fell into the hands of robbers. They stripped him of his clothes, beat him and went away, leaving him half dead. A priest happened to be going down the same road, and when he saw the man, he passed by on the other side. So too, a Levite, when he came to the place and saw him, passed by on the other side. But a Samaritan,*

as he traveled, came where the man was; and when he saw him, he took pity on him. He went to him and bandaged his wounds, pouring on oil and wine. Then he put the man on his own donkey, took him to an inn and took care of him. The next day he took out two silver coins and gave them to the innkeeper. 'Look after him,' he said, 'and when I return, I will reimburse you for any extra expense you may have.'

"Which of these three do you think was a neighbour to the man who fell into the hands of robbers?"

The expert in the law replied, "The one who had mercy on him."

Jesus told him, "Go and do likewise." Luke 10:30-37 New International Version

Do you realize how much money that the Samaritan paid to take care of that injured man? Could you afford to find somebody on the street and pay for 3 meals a day for 7 days, plus a hotel room for 7 days? Now add to that the high price of United States hospital charges too! In Luke you can read that it was all paid in cash. In order to pay all of that, you need to have abundance. Read again verse 37 which exhorts us to *"Go and do likewise"*. How many of us are financially capable of going and doing likewise?

Name your seed. Don't just throw your seed to anybody, but sow your seed intentionally. Plant it so you can get a harvest. Name your harvest. When a farmer plants his crops he knows what he is expecting to harvest. A farmer does not plant carrot seeds and then expect lettuce to arise. He knows what is supposed to spring up. After all, there is only one way to get a harvest and that is to plant a seed. If you have a need, then go plant a seed.

I will not ask you to do what I myself have not already done and continue to do. Your harvest might not come same day that you sow your seed. You need to be patient and believe the Word of God no matter the circumstances. The Word of God says as you will have the harvest if you do not give up. The Word works, but you have to work the Word.

I do not give finances to ministries because I feel sorry for them or feel that if I don't give, they will go under. I sow into ministries where the soil is producing.

Sowing into ministries that desperately need it is known as alms. Alms is giving to the poor and is something we should do, but it is not considered tithes nor offerings so the harvest on it is different. If a ministry is desperate, perhaps it is because they aren't doing what they are supposed to be doing.

Let us go back to the analogy of a farmer for a minute. A farmer is not likely to put seed into horrible, pitiful soil.. A farmer doesn't put a seed into the ground because he feels sorry for the ground. He sows because he is expecting his harvest to come up.

God is not in Heaven pacing back and forth while wringing His hands wondering how to get you the finances you need. He is not covered in sweat and anxiety concerning your economic future. He has neither mortgaged those pearly gates nor sold the pearly gates to make ends meet. Almighty God has not laid-off any angels because He has run out of resources. He wants you to know that He is still Almighty and still on the Throne! He is not controlled by the stock exchange or the price of a barrel of oil. The kingdom of God is not in a financial crisis.

> "`Give, and it will be given to you. They will pour
> into your lap a good measure - pressed down, shaken
> together, and running over. For by your standard of

measure it will be measured to you in return." Luke
6:38 New American Standard Bible

That verse does not say that you should be a giver and just hope for the best. The Word of God stated plainly in Luke, *"give and it will be given unto you…"* Make no apology for the blessing of God operating in your life. God Himself put that spiritual law into motion. We all have the same access into the blessing as the same spiritual laws are at work in your life also.

> *"This book of the law shall not depart out of thy mouth; but thou shalt meditate therein day and night, that thou mayest observe to do according to all that is written therein: for then thou shalt make thy way prosperous, and then thou shalt have good success." Joshua 1:8 King James Version*

Everyone can agree that the words "prosperous" and "success" includes the area of finances. We just read in Joshua to study God's Word and obey it. If you do what scripture says, then you will be prosperous and have success. Notice that Joshua 1:8 includes the words "for then," which indicates a promise that it is conditional. We must do our part for it to come to pass. We know God is faithful and will always do His part. God's love is unconditional but His promises are conditional and often connected to a principle.

CHAPTER 4: WHAT GIVES GOD PLEASURE

"Beloved, I wish above all things that thou mayest prosper and be in health, even as thy soul prospereth." 3 John 2:1 King James Version (KJV)

Jehovah's favourite and biggest desire for the church is that we would be in health and prosper. That verse alone should tell you that He really doesn't want us sick, broke, or lacking anything. Prosperity does not start with what is in your savings account. It begins with revelation knowledge of scripture such as 3 John 2. Revelation of scripture starts changing you and that change manifests itself in your bank account.

"Let them shout for joy and rejoice, who favor my vindication; And let them say continually, "The Lord be magnified, Who takes delight in the prosperity of His servant." Psalm 35:27 New American Standard Bible

He takes delight (pleasure) in prospering those that are serving Him. You can not watch secular television all day, every day while expecting God to just drop money on you like He is some type of Santa Clause. Give the Lord pleasure today by serving Him together with being open to receive His blessings!!

If God could only bless you financially when the world economics are doing well, then how would that show that He is God? He specializes in giving you abundance during a time when others are in famine. After all, He is The Way Maker. The economy does not dictate your bank account. Your obedience to the Word of God alone dictates your bank account. God is bigger and far above the economy of the earth.

> *"But you shall remember the Lord your God, for it is He who is giving you power to make wealth, that He may confirm His covenant which He swore to your fathers, as it is this day." Deuteronomy 8:18 New American Standard Version*

If wealth was so wrong, why would God give you the ability to get it? God gives you the strength, ingenuity, and health to get wealth. It has nothing to do with politicians. He will give you the ability to get out of bed and the ideas and connections you need. He never says that the lazy will have money fall from the sky onto them! God's method of getting seed for you to sow may require you getting off the couch.

Whether you are wealthy or not has nothing to do with your government. It has nothing to do with the president, prime-minister, price of gasoline or healthcare. God is the one who gives you the ability to get wealth.

> *"And it shall be, when the LORD thy God shall have brought thee into the land which he sware unto thy fathers, to Abraham, to Isaac, and to Jacob, to give thee great and goodly cities, which thou buildedst not,*
>
> *And houses full of all good things, which thou filledst not, and wells digged, which thou diggedst not, vineyards and olive trees, which thou plantedst not; when*

thou shalt have eaten and be full;" Deuteronomy
6:10 – 11 King James Version (KJV)

It is not what you read in the Bible that matters, it is what you read and obey that will assist you! You can believe that the giving of tithes and offerings is Biblical and still neglect doing it. If you feel like Heaven is brass and your prayers are not getting through, you need to ask the Lord where it is that you need to be obedient. Ask Him what the blessing blocker is. The problem is never with God. He is not holding blessings back from you.

> *"For the Lord God is a sun and shield: The Lord will give grace and glory: no good thing will He withhold from them that walk uprightly." Psalm 84:11 King James Version*

Give and do not withhold. When you give, there is not merely a possibility that it will be given back to you. The bible says that it WILL be given back unto you.

> *"Give, and it shall be given unto you; good measure, pressed down, and shaken together, and running over, shall men give into your bosom. For with the same measure that ye mete withal it shall be measured to you again." Luke 6:38 King James Version*

When you go to a grocery store and want to go home with some merchandise, you exchange money in order to take merchandise out of the store. If you did not pay for the product you are taking home, that would be called shoplifting.

If you eat at a restaurant I am sure that you pay the bill. It is the same with when someone serves you up some good preaching. You dine at the table of listening to preachers serve up a good message (by the way this book alone took over 100 hours). Yes, the gospel is free, but the man or woman of God still need their bills paid. Preparing a good sermon takes hours and hours. Pastors and evangelists deserve an income.

> *"The one who is taught the word is to share all good*
> *things with the on who teaches him." Galatians 6:6*
> New American Standard Bible

When I did prison ministry for three years I needed a decent vehicle that worked. In addition I required gasoline, insurance, and clothes on my back in order to minister to the inmates. Let me tell you that it is much easier sharing the gospel with people when you don't have to be concerned about finances, but are able to just concentrate on kingdom advancement! The gospel is free but getting evangelists to the four corners of the earth certainly is not.

Your giving controls your income. The Bible states that when we give it will be given back to us running over.

God will not violate His own economic laws set out in His Word. You give sparingly to the work of God then you will reap sparingly. *You determine your financial future* with these spiritual laws. Your boss at work does not determine your financial future.

God does not need your money. He is using money to test your obedience. Money is so incredibly powerful, that it can easily be used to show you the condition of your heart. Take a good look at your bank statement as to where you have spent your money, and it will loudly show you where your treasure is. What you do with money is a testament of who you are. If you give sparingly, God will give it back to you in an eyedropper. When you give, you are not choosing what God gets, you are choosing what you get to reap in harvest.

> *"And they said unto Him, We have here but five*
> *loaves, and two fishes.*

He said, Bring them hither to me.

And He commanded the multitude to sit down on the grass, and took the five loaves, and the two fishes, and looking up to Heaven, He blessed, and brake, and gave the loaves to His disciples, and the disciples to the multitude. And they did all eat, and were filled: and they took up of the fragments that remained twelve baskets full. And they that had eaten were about five thousand men, beside women and children." Matthew 14:17-21 King James Version

Matthew 14:17-21 is the account of the boy with the loaves and the fishes. It shows us in no uncertain terms that when we offer what we have to God, He multiplies it. Our little is much in the hands of God. At this very moment, you may not have a lot to give, but you certainly have something that you can present to the Lord. We read in that passage in Matthew that 5,000 men, plus their women and children were fed on a two piece fish dinner! There easily could have been 15,000 people fed if you add all the men, women and children! We must stop looking at what we don't have, but give to God what we do have. Everyone has something in their hands that they can sow as seed.

It probably took just one basket for the boy to bring his lunch to the meeting that day. There were 12 baskets left over! I just like to think that the boy was allowed to bring those 12 baskets back home and say, "Momma. I went with my lunch in one basket. I offered it to the disciples of Jesus, and it multiplied. It fed 15,000 and I'm bringing 12 baskets back to you!" When you turn loose what is in your hand to God, He will turn loose what is in His hand for you. What you make happen with others, God will make happen for you.

You might bring to the church meeting one basket, help 15,000, AND come home with 12 baskets because our God is like that! If you will release what is in your hand that you say is good, and give it to God, He will exchange it for something *better*. That requires trusting God and letting go of what you have before what God gives in return arrives into your hands. That is called living by faith. That means you need to take Him at His Word. Act and react like the Bible is true. It is only after you have fully released that which is good to Him that He exchanges it for something better. Then later you can do an exchange again. You can give it to the work of God and believe God to exchange your seed into a mighty harvest every single time because that is the nature and character of God. That means that you have to be without fear of lack. You have to release what you have to God knowing that you will always be taken care of. You have to be excited and comfortable in those moments between the release of the seed and the time when the harvest comes in.

As I have mentioned, the 30 or 60 or 100 fold return does not always come to you in the mail the same day that you release the seed. Sometimes the harvest takes time to grow. Do not allow yourself to entertain any evil thoughts of unbelief.

> *"Take heed, brethren, lest there be in any of you and evil heart of unbelief, in departing from the living God." Hebrews 3:12 King James Version.*

God said that if you give, you will get a harvest. That settles it once and for all. He will not lie to you. His Word is true.

> *"Give, and it will be given to you. They will pour into your lap a good measure - pressed down, shaken together, and running over. For by your standard of measure it will be measured to you in return. Luke 6:38 New American Standard Bible*

If you give nothing, the return on that is a harvest of nothing. It honestly is that plain and simple.

> Bring ye all the tithes into the storehouse, that there may be meat in mine house, and prove me now herewith, saith the LORD of hosts, if I will not open you the windows of heaven, and pour you out a blessing, that there shall not be room enough to receive it. And I will rebuke the devourer for your sakes, and he shall not destroy the fruits of your ground; neither shall your vine cast her fruit before the time in the field, saith the LORD of hosts.
>
> And all nations shall call you blessed: for ye shall be a delightsome land, saith the LORD of hosts."
> Malichi 3:10 King James Version

The Bible says we can have the windows of Heaven opened over our bank accounts! Do you want there to be so much put into your hands that you could share with neighbours, missionaries, and churches? Wouldn't you like to be in need of storage units because you do not have room enough in your house to receive it? If you have room to receive more then you are not at that place yet.

We all want the devourer, who is also called the Devil, to be rebuked off of our finances. We want nations to call us blessed because it is so obvious the Lord's favour is on us. All of that is contained in Malachi 3:10-12 and it is also all conditional. Meet your part of the conditions of this spiritual law of kingdom finances, and God will do His part. No fear here. If God tells me to give an offering, then I will be obedient immediately.

God wants you to be aware of where your faith is and what level of trust you have in Him.

CHAPTER 5 YOUR GIVING AS A MEMORIAL

*He saw in a vision evidently about the ninth hour
of the day an angel of God coming in to him, and
saying unto him, Cornelius. And when he looked on
him, he was afraid, and said, What is it, Lord? And
he said unto him, Thy prayers and thine alms are
come up for a memorial before God. Acts 10: 3 – 4
King James Version*

Did you know that your giving creates a memorial? Cornelius'
alms came up before the Lord.

God Himself couldn't forget what just happened. Heaven
itself took note of Cornelius' giving. Immediately angels got
dispatched. Peter was sent to the gentiles to preach to them the
gospel after this time of praying and giving. Cornelius' alms came
up as a memorial before God. Have you given something that God
is still thinking about? Is Heaven talking about your giving?

God gave His best for you at the cross. Because of His love for
the world, He gave (John 3:16). What have we given back to Him
in response? Again, it's not what you believe that is important,
but it is what you will *obey and act* on that makes the difference.
Faith without works is dead. If you do what God is telling you to

do, then you will have what God has said that you can have. The choice is in your hands. You can't sit back and say "If God wants to bless me, He will bless me." He's waiting on you, so don't blame God if things don't go well.

> "Death and life are in the power of the tongue: and they that love it shall eat the fruit thereof." Proverbs 18:21 King James Version

The Word of God says in Proverbs 18:21 that the choice of life or death is in OUR tongue. It isn't even up to the devil.

> "For even in Thessalonica you sent [me contributions] for my needs, not only once but a second time. Not that I seek or am eager for [your] gift, but I do seek and am eager for the fruit which increases to your credit [the harvest of blessing that is accumulating to your account]." Philippians 4:16,17 Amplified Bible

We are giving so that the gospel of Jesus Christ goes out. The spreading the gospel to change lives is His highest priority. The Bible tells us that He is not willing that any should perish.

> "At destruction and famine thou shalt laugh: neither shalt thou be afraid of the beasts of the earth." Job 5:22 King James Version

You don't need to worry about famine. You don't need to worry about the economy. If you are focused on the gospel, God will focus on you. He wants a people that look like Him, talk like Him, love like Him, and give like Him.

> "A good man leaveth an inheritance to his children's children: and the wealth of the sinner is laid up for the just." Proverbs 13:22 King James Version

No money nor gold has been taken off of the earth. It is all still there, but just perhaps in fewer hands. God has spiritual laws that will bring it into your hands. I read that a trillion dollars or more will change hands in 2013. I am in line! I am giving tithes and offerings so I won't be passed by. The poverty of the sinner is not going to be given to the righteous, but the wealth. The wealth of the sinner is finances.

If you are offered something that you already have one of (such as a new car), you should accept that item as given by God. You can then either sell the extra car and sow the money, or directly sow the car into someone's life. Get alone with God and ask Him what you are to do with it. One of the mandates of the church is to be a Holy Spirit guided distribution center for money and other resources. There is a single mom or a preacher that needs a nice car, so just go watch their face light up when you give it to them!

These scriptures need to go from just information to being revelation so it can then bring manifestation. Without revelation knowledge regarding finances, you will never enjoy your full inheritance.

> *"The rich ruleth over the poor, and the borrower is servant to the lender." Proverbs 22:7 King James Version*

According to Genesis, we have come to rule, not to be ruled over. Scripture says we are to subdue the Earth. So we know that we should be a people that do not borrow because the lender is ruler over the borrower.

> *"Owe no man any thing, but to love one another: for he that loveth another hath fulfilled the law." Romans 13:8 King James Version*

CHAPTER 6: JESUS WAS NOT BROKE

"For you know the grace of our Lord Jesus Christ, that though he was rich, yet for your sakes he became poor, so that you through his poverty might become rich." 2 Corinthians 8:9 New International Version (NIV)

There is a wrong teaching that Jesus was broke and that to be holy, we should be broke also. I believe the "poor" spoken of in 2 Corinthians 8:9 refers to His leaving Heaven to be on earth for a time. Let's look at a few scriptures that suggest that Jesus was not broke.

First of all, the Bible tells us that His garment was a seamless one. That means it was not a cheap rag.

" Then the soldiers, when they had crucified Jesus, took his garments, and made four parts, to every soldier a part; and also his coat: now the coat was without seam, woven from the top throughout. They said therefore among themselves, Let us not rend it, but cast lots for it, whose it shall be: that the scripture might be fulfilled, which saith, They parted my raiment among them, and for my vesture they did

cast lots. These things therefore the soldiers did. "
John 19:23-24 King James Version

Second point just on those two verses in John is the fact that the soldiers cast lots for his garments at the foot of the cross. They are not going to gamble for rags. So religious people are just going to have to deal with the fact that He wore nice clothing.

Jesus also needed an accountant. Why would Jesus need His treasurer, Judas, to keep track of the money if he only had two cents?

Jesus became sin so that we could become righteous. Most of us can accept that. We have been taught that about Jesus and are comfortable with that statement.

> *" For He hath made Him to be sin for us, who knew no sin; that we might be made the righteousness of God in Him." 2 Corinthians 5:21*

Jesus took stripes on His back so that we could become healed. Most of us can accept that.

> *"But He was wounded for our transgressions, He was bruised for our iniquities: the chastisement of our peace was upon Him; and with His stripes we were healed." Isaiah 53:5 King James Version*

We love that verse in Isaiah and many of us can easily quote it.

But, do you also realize that He also became poor so that we could be made rich?

> *"For ye know the grace of our Lord Jesus Christ, that, though he was rich, yet for your sakes he became poor, that ye through his poverty might*

become rich." 2 Corinthians 8:9 American Standard Version

Are you full of vision and purpose to expand the kingdom of God or are you consumed with your budget? I have asked Him for big stuff to get this end-time harvest. I believe that He is going to expand my budget to meet the vision. Be vision minded and full of faith for the budget. Just be a witness for Him as that is putting the kingdom of God first place. So many of us make most of our decisions based on what is in our bank account instead of based on the Word of God. I will move ahead with vision from God because he is pro(for) vision. He will provide the provision. If he tells you to do something, He will make sure it is paid for. Make sure you do your part to hear and obey. When you do that, then all things that you have need of will be added to you. Don't let someone come along and give you a guilt trip about being blessed. Smile and let them know that it is simply things being added to you according to Matthew 6:33

> *"Seek first His kingdom and His righteousness, and all these things will be added to you." Matthew 6:33 New American Standard Bible*

Consume yourself with the Kingdom of God advancing, and He will make sure that you are taken care of.

We have to learn to hear and obey. We need to give the amount that God has told to you to give. If we aren't giving correctly, then how could we ask God to bless our bank account? That would be asking Him to sanction disobedience.

Do not give because of emotion or pressure from any preacher, but give because of conviction of the Holy Spirit. The Holy Spirit will never go crossways to the Word of God.

"Give, and it will be given to you. A good measure, pressed down, shaken together and running over, will be poured into your lap. For with the measure you use, it will be measured to you." Luke 6:38 New International Version

I know that verse was quoted earlier but need to bring it up again. This next scripture does not instruct us to hoard or hold back from the Lord because of a fear of lack. If you have fear, then your love walk is not perfected yet.

"There is no fear in love. But, perfect love drives out fear, because hear has to do with punishment. The one who fears is not made perfect in love." 1 John 4:18 New International Version

Each time you give, there is a spiritual law in effect. You can take it to the bank that your harvest will be coming in. Plant enough and you may just have a harvest coming in daily! I don't want to be known as someone who was just mediocre or boring. I want to live boldly and never be lukewarm. There is a lot to get done, church! I am going big before I go home!

"Now faith is the substance of things hoped for, the evidence of things not seen." Hebrews 11:1 King James Version

One of the meanings of "evidence" in original Greek is "title deed." In legal terms, a title deed is proof that you own something. Faith is the proof that you own something that has not even manifested yet. We need to truly believe that we have title deed to a harvest with our name on it. Do not walk right past your harvest because you do not even recognize it. Build up your discernment and spiritual muscles so you can pull your harvest from the spiritual realm into the seen realm. Your fruitful harvest will die on the vine if you do not have knowledge of what is yours. Remember Hosea 4:6 that people perish from lack of knowledge.

If it is wrong for a Christian to have money then how would we pay for a church building to meet in? Does it give God glory and make Him sound like a good Father when His people file for bankruptcy or foreclosure? Now, I am not talking about spending way beyond your income. Follow His wisdom and leading. We can no longer do our own thing and ask God to bless it.

In order to have a harvest, seed has to be put into the ground. Then you have to let the seed do its thing. The seed already has inside of it the ability to spring up in the right conditions. An apple seed already has the right make-up inside of it for a harvest if the soil conditions are correct. Tithe has to be given to good ground.

If you haven't been faithful in your tithes, offerings and alms then just repent and make a quality decision before God to get back on track.

> *"A time to be born, and a time to die; and a time to pluck up that which is planted."* Ecclesiastes 3:2
> King James Version

Of course we are all excited about the harvest time. The reality is that it all starts with letting go of the seed out of your hand and putting it into good soil.

> *"Verily, verily, I say unto you, Except a corn of wheat falls into the ground and die, it abideth alone: but if it die, it bringeth forth much fruit."* John 12:24
> King James Version

Money seed means money harvest. A farmer does not plant corn and expect apples to come up. If you want a financial harvest then a financial seed is required. You don't want your dollar to be alone. You don't want it to abide alone but be multiplied many times over which is the "much fruit" spoken of in John 12:24.

Jesus is returning again and that return is very soon. We have a lot to do before we leave this earth. He may come back during our lifetime. Regardless of when He returns, we only have one lifetime to advance the kingdom of God with the resources entrusted to us! Perhaps you are unable go travel to another country right now as a missionary, but you can support one. You can support missionaries with your finances so that the work they do for the kingdom will also be credited to your Heavenly account. Yes, souls that are saved and the lives that are changed as a result of the minister you supported financially will definitely your reward also.

Those who are called by Almighty God to preach the gospel, desperately need to get dedicated to doing what they are called to do. Those who are called by God to finance the gospel, desperately need to get doing what they are called to do.

SECTION TWO: BREAKTHROUGH FASTING

CHAPTER 7 NOTHING
ELSE SATISFIES

"Blessed are they who do hunger and thirst after righteousness, for they shall be filled." Matthew 5:6 King James Version

Maturity and breakthrough comes when we hunger and thirst for God and for His righteousness more than we hunger and thirst for anything else. I promise you that secular television programming, with all of its reality shows , can not compare with time with Him. Nothing else satisfies like time in His presence. Besides, I have never received any deep revelation from Him while watching secular television. I am not saying that it is sin to watch television. However, I do believe that if you are desperate to advance the kingdom of God, you need to spend your time with Him. If you are in need of some wisdom from the Holy Spirit in order to navigate through a particular situation, then you need to spend time hearing from Heaven!

How big is your hunger for more of Him? If there are things that you have been praying for and believing for that have not manifested yet, fasting will bring those things to fruition. It just makes sense that we would want to spend time hearing from the One who has all the wisdom! If you are experiencing blockages to your blessings that are promised in the Word of God, then utilize fasting to help you hear how to remove those blockages. The Commander-in-Chief is very willing to share clearly with you what the blockages to your breakthrough are.

It is vitally important to let the Lord speak. When I am spending time in prayer and fasting, I am not the one doing all the talking. So many times we use our prayer time doing all the talking and then walk away as if we were all done praying. Meanwhile, the completely wise Holy Spirit would like you to hear the answers to all the questions you have for Him. Please do not ask Him a bunch of questions then end your prayer time without letting Him get a word in edgewise. He has all the answers you are looking for. During fasting the emphasis should be strengthening your spiritual ears to hear. It's a precious time developing the relationship with Him to another level.

Every time you press into Him, there are insights and breakthroughs that you just can not receive any other way.

If you are frustrated with your life and know that there must be deeper, better, and higher places to go with the Lord, then I know what I want you to do! Replace frustration with fasting.

We all want to have an alive, vibrant, progressive walk with the Lord. When I start to feel things becoming stale and "same old –same old," or when I need a fresh encounter with God, fasting is one of the major tools I use. Times of frustration are not always because of being in sin. Sometimes frustration occurs because of precious hunger for more of Him. I use the word "frustration" but it might also be understood as dissatisfaction. My desire for more of His Kingdom here on earth grew so big, that I was not satisfied with where I was at. It took me a little while to discern what it was that I was feeling and dealing with. Not many preachers teach about this. These same preachers do not understand why some in their congregation are experiencing dissatisfaction. When people experience dissatisfaction, it may be projected on others instead of realizing it has to do with their relationship with God.

I went through a time where I just knew there were additional revelations about prayer that I could learn. Then I realized that in order to have what I have not had before, I had to do what I had not done before. So, I decided that I was going to spend an hour a day, every day, in deliberate fellowship with Him.

We all want to live under an open Heaven with hell shut. With much confidence I feel safe in saying we want all of our enemy's plans thwarted. Fasting includes opening ourselves for strategy, knowledge, wisdom, and revelation. That means time, in the presence of the Lord with all other noise removed.

In some ways it may feel like you are not making progress and that you are just spinning your wheels financially, spiritually, and even physically. Make a quality decision to press into God for all He has for you. A quality decision is one from which you refuse to change or retreat from.

Are you content with where you are at spiritually, financially, and with your health? Even if your health, finances and relationships are doing well right now, there is always more ground to take spiritually. We could never, on this earth, know and experience all there is about Jehovah God. If you are still alive and breathing, then there is more you can do to advance the kingdom of God. As long as there is one unsaved person on this earth, there is work we can do and therefore, divine strategy needed to be downloaded to us from the Holy Spirit. Put yourself in a position to hear Him. Put your self in a posture, on purpose, to hear Him.

When we leave this earth and have our home-going back to heaven, I wonder if God will show us what our life could have been if we would have just spent less time watching television?

Too much time is wasted on doing things that don't effect eternity at all.

I don't know if Jesus is returning while I am on this earth, or if I will go to Heaven by way of the grave. The signs certainly point to the fact that He could come at any second. Regardless of how you leave this earth, you and I only have our one lifetime on this earth to complete our calling and our assignment from Heaven. Millions would go to Hell if He were to appear today to take believers home with Him. Seriously let that sink in. Hell is real and millions still have not received Jesus as Lord and Saviour.

There is so much vision inside me sometimes and it appears as if very little is happening on the outside. I can get a bit frustrated over how long things appear to be taking. Like everyone, I would like God to hurry up concering those which I have been praying into. It is important to realize here that prayer and fasting is not always an instant fix. Jesus is Lord, not Santa Clause. He knows if you just want Him solely for material things. He knows if you are after His hand or His face. I know He wants us prosperous and have experienced time and time again that when you seek His face, His hand is attached and close by.

Here is the most known scriptures about fasting found in Matthew chapter 6.

> *Matthew 6:TAKE CARE not to do your good deeds publicly or before men, in order to be seen by them; otherwise you will have no reward [reserved for and awaiting you] with and from your Father Who is in heaven.*

> *Thus, whenever you give to the poor, do not blow a trumpet before you, as the hypocrites in the synagogues and in the streets like to do, that they may be*

recognized and honoured and praised by men. Truly I tell you, they have their reward in full already.

But when you give to charity, do not let your left hand know what your right hand is doing,

So that your deeds of charity may be in secret; and your Father Who sees in secret will reward you openly.

Also when you pray, you must not be like the hypocrites, for they love to pray standing in the synagogues and on the corners of the streets, that they may be seen by people. Truly I tell you, they have their reward in full already.

But when you pray, go into your [most] private room, and, closing the door, pray to your Father, Who is in secret; and your Father, Who sees in secret, will reward you in the open.

And when you pray, do not heap up phrases (multiply words, repeating the same ones over and over) as the Gentiles do, for they think they will be heard for their much speaking. [I Kings 18:25-29.]

Do not be like them, for your Father knows what you need before you ask Him.

NOW DOWN TO VERSE 16

And whenever you are fasting, do not look gloomy and sour and dreary like the hypocrites, for they put on a dismal countenance, that their fasting may be apparent to and seen by men. Truly I say to you, they have their reward in full already.

But when you fast, perfume your head and wash your face,

So that your fasting may not be noticed by men but by your Father, Who sees in secret; and your Father, Who sees in secret, will reward you in the open. Matthew 6: 1-8, 16 - 18 Amplified Version

God wants to reward you. Matthew 6:6 that we just read clearly states that your Father will reward you. It does not say that He might reward you. It says so straight-forward in verse 18 that His heart is to give rewards. However, there is no reward if you do your fasting piously. Verse 18 also states that He will reward your fasting, praying, and giving when you do it for an audience of one (Him). That passage of scripture in Matthew 6 also tells us that if you get your reward with men, then your Heavenly Father doesn't have to give reward.

I am here to please God and not men. Everything that I do is to minister to Him. He doesn't want meaningless repetition or rote. He doesn't want us doing the motions of church. You can do all the church related activities without any power.

"Having a form of godliness, but denying the power thereof: from such turn away." 2 Timothy 3:5 King James Version

Fasting illuminates areas that need growth so we can grow and live our lives on the next higher level. The world is waiting for us to move in power.

CHAPTER 8: WHEN YOU FAST

"Deep calls to deep in the roar of your waterfalls;
all your waves and breakers have swept over me."
Psalms 42:7 New International Version

When you are fasting and praying, you do not have to offer a long, King James Version of the Bible sounding prayer in order for angels to respond with their assistance. There is nothing wrong with the King James type of English or praying at length, but those two things are not requirements for an effective prayer to be heard and answered. In Daniel chapter ten, we read an account between an angel and Daniel.

"Then he continued, "Do not be afraid, Daniel. Since the first day that you set your mind to gain under-standing and to humble yourself before your God, your words were heard, and I have come in response to them" Daniel 10:12 New International Version

"Be not therefore like unto them; for your Father knoweth what things ye have need of, before ye ask Him." Matthew 6:8 King James Version

That scripture in Matthew 6 does not mean that we are not allowed to ask the Lord anything. He is talking about the attitude and piety during prayer. We need to take the whole counsel of God and not just one scripture out of context.

> *"You desire but do not have, so you kill. You covet but you cannot get what you want, so you quarrel and fight. You do not have because you do not ask God." James 4:2 New International Version*

The Bible says in James 4:2 KJV that we are allowed to come to God with our requests. Since scripture will not contradict or go against scripture then Matthew 6:8 certainly could be referring to the fact we do not need to repeat ourselves to be heard. God is not deaf. Let the One who has all the answers do some of the talking and don't do all the talking all of the time.

God wants things on earth to be done as it is in Heaven. There is no sickness or poverty in Heaven! He wants us to have some Heaven on Earth NOW. He has not laid-off any angels, nor mortgaged the Pearly Gates because there is a recession in Heaven. He wants our prayers to be that we would be experiencing right now, on Earth, as it is in Heaven. Therefore I pray like God wants things on Earth to be as glorious as it is in Heaven.

> *"Moreover when ye fast, be not, as the hypocrites, of a sad countenance: for they disfigure their faces, that they may appear unto men to fast. Verily I say unto you, They have their reward." Matthew 6:16 King James Version*

The Bible says "when" you fast, not "if" you fast. That tells us that our Heavenly Father expects fasting to be a part of a believer's life.

There are parts of the Bible that speaks to the Jews. Then there are parts of the Bible that were written to the church and lastly are the parts written to unbelievers. When there is a scripture that was written for the church (assuming you are saved), then read it out loud and insert your name. He expects (insert your name here) to fast and when (insert your name here) does, He will reward (insert your name here).

> *"As the deer pants for streams of water, so my soul pants for you, my God. My soul thirsts for God, for the living God. When can I go and meet with God?"*
> *Psalms 42:1-2 New International Version*

I am panting and wanting God more than anything! I want time with Him. I want to hang out together with Him more than anything. I find it hard sometimes to go get groceries or to even make dinner because all I want is to lock myself away with Him. But, I am getting better at communing with Him at deeper levels even while I am getting everything done during the day. Everyone still needs to shower and do laundry. We all need to work and take care of our families. When you have precious children, they absolutely need you to invest in them.

I am learning to keep a high consciousness of God with my spirit open to Him in prayer even when I am doing essential activities that things that have to get accomplished. God is the one who ultimately decided there was to be 24 hours in each day. Jehovah God, who orchestrated the whole universe and continues to administrate it, can show us how to plan our time. It's a matter of disciplining ourselves to tune our spirits to Him no matter what we are doing. We also must set aside dedicated time for prayer with nothing else going on.

We human beings are so used to listening to people talk with our natural ears. Some people have grown up with the television on for many, many hours a day and have gone far away from living in the spirit realm. If you truly pant after Him, then you'll do what it takes to hang out with Him. My schedule revolves around time with Him. I am not just fitting Him into my schedule. He is too important to be last. My schedule fits around Him.

Fasting is not just giving up a few meals or forgoing dessert. That is known as a diet. Fasting is because you have a *specific, spiritual purpose*. The whole reason for participating in a fast is to have more of Him which in turn equates to more breakthrough for you! If you are not going to replace food with more of Him, then the results of fasting will be lacking.

I want to hear Him more. I can remember one particular Sunday when the Lord was moving with Words of Knowledge. I was praying for people and prophetic words were flowing. It was such a holy time that I didn't want to mess it up with my flesh at all. My plea was to have the Lord direct everything. Fasting tunes God's voice in so much more.

If you want to develop your spiritual ear muscles, then you have to use them. Just like getting in shape in the natural, if you want to get in shape spiritually it will take purposeful effort and purposeful activities to develop spiritual muscles. Body builders do not sit on the couch eating empty calories and expect muscles to appear on their body. If they want upper body strength, they work the upper body. If you want to hear the leading of the Lord with more clarity, then intentionally work on that. Everything else becomes quieter and His voice will become clearer as you abide in Him. Be consciously aware of the voice of the Holy Spirit. Abiding in Him requires that He is where you reside, not just visit periodically in a crisis. Do you forget about Him when times are good?

The whole purpose for fasting is to hear God more and get the clutter out. If you want to have that radar developed to pick up on what God is doing and saying, then fasting will do just that.

Start contending for some breakthroughs for yourself. Are you asking others to do the praying for you? Yes, we are to pray for each other. My point is that you do not make it the sole responsibility of others to do all the contending in the spirit realm for you. Some people just don't want to put much effort in and are happy to continually ask others to pray for them while never doing much prayer themselves. It's time to grow up, precious church, and not be in the same situation next year as you are this year.

Matthew 6 does say "when" you give, and "when" you fast and "when" you pray. He does completely expect that praying, giving, and fasting are part of a believer's life. Matthew 6 does not say "if you fast," or "if I could interrupt your television time for a minute." Matthew 6 is pretty direct in saying *when* you fast, because it was not a nice little suggestion. God is direct in the Bible when communicating what will bring you breakthrough. Mature Christianity means God's commandments and instructions in the Bible are not received as mere suggestions.

The devil knows that fasting is a major weapon against him, so he will try to keep you too busy and extremely tired in order to hinder your spiritual growth. The devil doesn't mind if you are in church three days a week. He doesn't mind at all if you are so busy, even if it is with good things. He just wants to make sure that you don't have time for serious soul winning or bearing much fruit (John 15:8). The devil wants you busy, not fruitful. He gets nervous when you *are the church* and go outside the four walls of a church building sharing the gospel. Apply what you learned at church from Monday all the way to the following Sunday and continue applying what you learn from the Word for the rest of your life. Go get built up and strengthened with the body of believers and then go take it with you everywhere you go.

Like many others, I am on a social media site, check e-mails, and also text message people. Then it hit me that I can be so busy communicating with other people, that I neglect communicating with God.

We do not need to attend another "pump you up conference" where the "high" lasts a few days but nothing in your life has honestly changed. Are all the activities which you are participating in at church assisting you in fulfilling the great commission?

Where is the boldness to go and lead others to Christ? Fast and pray for the divine rearranging of your schedule and priorities.

> *"Then saith he unto his disciples, The harvest truly is plenteous, but the labourers are few; Pray ye therefore the Lord of the harvest, that he will send forth labourers into his harvest." Matthew 9:37-38 King James Version*

The harvest of souls ready to receive Jesus as Lord and Saviour is plentiful, but the workers are few. Therefore, the issue is not with the harvest, it is with the lack of workers. We need a conference where the focus is denying our flesh, getting with God and hearing from Him instructions for the harvest. We need lasting growth and change. We are supposed to be ruling, reigning and subduing the earth (Genesis 1: 28 KJV). Instead, some of us are leading defeated lives.

We need to take the time to be in God's presence in prayer and fasting so that we are full of Him. People should be able to see and know there is something different about us.

> *"Wherefore come out from among them, and be ye separate, saith the Lord, and touch not the unclean thing; and I will receive you." 2 Corinthians 6:17*

If you want strength to help you to not act like the world, then a fast will help. If you want the Holy Spirit to reveal to you things that you are doing that are hindering kingdom advancement, then a fast will start the revealing and healing of those things. We don't always realize what things the Lord would like to remove from our lives until they are revealed during a fast.

A famous story that mentions fasting is in Matthew 17. It is the story of a father who had a demon-possessed son. As the son grew older, the attacks became so severe that the boy would throw himself into an open fire or a trench of water. A suicidal spirit tormented this boy constantly. The situation became extremely serious. The disciples couldn't help the boy. Why? Perhaps it was because they weren't prayed up.

> *"Lord, have mercy on my son," he said. "He has seizures and is suffering greatly. He often falls into the fire or into the water. I brought him to your disciples, but they could not heal him."*
>
> *"You unbelieving and perverse generation," Jesus replied, "how long shall I stay with you? How long shall I put up with you? Bring the boy here to me." Jesus rebuked the demon, and it came out of the boy, and he was healed at that moment. Matthew 17:15-18 New International Version*

Matthew 10:1 records that Jesus had already given the disciples power to cast out evil spirits and to heal every disease. Why couldn't the disciples, in an account just 7 chapters later, cast out the demon and cure the boy when they were given authority to do so?

> *"And Jesus said unto them, Because of your unbelief: for verily I say unto you, If ye have faith as a grain of mustard seed, ye shall say unto this mountain, Remove hence to yonder place; and it shall remove; and nothing shall be impossible unto you.*

21 Howbeit this kind goeth not out but by prayer and fasting." Matthew 17:20-21 King James Version

What bondages are yet unbroken because we have neglected to pray and fast? Notice the two go together in that verse of scripture. If you just go without food or something else for a period of time and don't replace that time with seeking God in prayer with all you have got, remember that is just a diet.

We love quoting from Matthew 17 mentioned above: "nothing shall be impossible unto you." However, we just can't isolate that part of the verse and ignore what it is tied to. We must pay attention to the next line of scripture in Matthew 17:21 and the word "howbeit". Howbeit is a connection and linking word connecting the part of scripture with a part that perhaps is not our favourite. Before *"nothing is impossible unto you,"* is prayer and fasting. God is willing to do His part, we have to do our part.

How many of us have successfully cast out a demon lately or been used of God in the area of healing? To accomplish what you have not accomplished before, you have to do what you haven't done before. Long before Jesus cast out of the demon from that boy that was being thrown into the fire, the Holy Spirit led Jesus into the wilderness to get away by Himself with God. Jesus spent forty days and forty nights taking no food (fasting). As a direct result, casting out that stubborn demon was not impossible for Jesus. He was all charged up from His time of prayer and fasting. If the Son of God knew that there were supernatural things that could only be released because of fasting, then how much more should fasting be a common occurrence in our lives? Jesus is our example in all things.

"And he said unto them, Can ye make the children of the bridechamber fast, while the bridegroom is

with them? But the days will come, when the bride-
groom shall be taken away from them, and then
shall they fast in those days." Luke 5:34-35 King
James Version

To say that you are pursuing God first and foremost, above everything, means that you are spending time in sweet fellowship with Him.

"But seek ye first the kingdom of God, and his righ-
teousness; and all these things shall be added unto
you." Matthew 6:33 King James Version

The Bible says in Matthew 6:33 to seek first the kingdom of God before you have everything you have need of being added unto you. If you need a place to live or if you need finances, then press into God with all you've got and what you need will be added unto. Make listening to Him a priority with fasting and prayer because He is the One with all the answers.

CHAPTER 9 WHEN FLESH
TAKES A BACK SEAT

When we think of fasting, Daniel chapter 10 commonly comes to mind. Daniel is quite known for fasting from certain foods. He fasted as he sought God. He was filled with wisdom and became second in command in the land. We read in Daniel 10:21 that Daniel fasted and as a result an angel was sent to assist him. Daniel's fast broke the power of the prince over Persia and released the angels of God so that God's purposes would be revealed.

Fasting makes your flesh (namely your stomach) take a back seat to the things of the spirit. It is not only possible, but also extremely advantageous, to have spiritual things more important than your stomach.

Food is mentioned a few times in scripture. I'm not going to expound on it too much but I will introduce these few scriptures here and let you "chew on it!" In Genesis we all know that Adam and Eve ate of the apple and immediately went from blissfully enjoying being in the presence of God to hiding from Him. Was that food worth it? Their stomachs were obviously temporarily satisfied, but what about their spirits? We need to lock our focus onto what affects eternity.

I have read about the sins of Sodom and Gomorrah as outlined in Ezekiel 16: 49, 50. The sermons I have heard on it usually focused on their rampant homosexuality, but there were other additional issues involved with it.

> "Behold, this was the guilt of your sister Sodom: she and her daughters had arrogance, abundant food and careless ease, but she did not help the poor and needy." Ezekiel 16:49-50 New American Standard Bible

With the people of Sodom, whatever their flesh wanted, they did. Is Jesus Lord over what you put in your mouth?

In Genesis we read the account of Jacob and Esau. Esau actually exchanged his birthright for food!

> "And Esau said, Behold, I am at the point to die: and what profit shall this birthright do to me? And Jacob said, Swear to me this day; and he sware unto him: and he sold his birthright unto Jacob. Then Jacob gave Esau bread and pottage of lentiles; and he did eat and drink, and rose up, and went his way: thus Esau despised his birthright." Genesis 25:32-34 King James Version

God had a plan for Esau's life, but his desire for food was greater than his desire for God's awesome plan. What have you missed out on because you exchanged destiny for instant gratification? Will you choose what God wants or what your flesh wants? I'm not saying that we are never to eat or enjoy something. That just is not the nature and character of God either. But, are you willing to fast from television to get more of God? Are you willing to go without some food or drink that you love for a period of time as a sign to God that He is more important? In Hebrews 12: 15-17 we read a warning against becoming like Esau.

"See that no one is sexually immoral, or is godless like Esau, who for a single meal sold his inheritance rights as the oldest son. 17 Afterward, as you know, when he wanted to inherit this blessing, he was rejected. Even though he sought the blessing with tears, he could not change what he had done."
Hebrews 12:16-17 New International Version

CHAPTER 10:
CORPORATE FASTING

Give God the first part of everything; the first part of every day, the first part of every week, the first part of every month, the first part of every year…. The number of churches that call a corporate fast is growing. Often this occurs in January to give God the first bit of the new year.

It is shocking to me and probably hurtful to the Holy Spirit that when a prayer meeting is called very few people show up. Hopefully that is not the case in your church. The Holy Spirit can be grieved. It just may be that He is grieved because He knows that prayer and fasting is such a massive key, yet people have apathetically neglected prayer and fasting. They would rather keep their problem instead of have a breakthrough I guess.

> *"And grieve not the holy Spirit of God, whereby ye are sealed unto the day of redemption." Ephesians 4:30 King James Version*

Remember Matthew 6:33 about seeking first the kingdom of God. If you want things added unto you, then you are going to have to do some active seeking. Seeking requires deliberate action. There is a strong possibility that the devil isn't going to sit calmly and respectfully and just let you fast without trying to distract you.

Your flesh certainly is going to want to kick and scream a bit. The stomach is used to ruling everything in your life. It is your spirit's turn to lead the way.

Some years ago now I completed a one year fast from junk-food. That might seem easy to some of you, but I had been eating chocolate and potato chips way too frequently. I wanted to hear His voice and leading more, so fasting was the key I found in the Bible as the way to a deeper leading of the Lord.

Previous to this fast, it was rare for someone to come and give me candy as a gift. But, during the year I fasted junk food so many people gave me boxes of chocolate that I was almost crying like a baby! Very few friends knew I was fasting because I don't announce it. I did stick to the quality decision that I made and spent the time reading my Bible and praying when I would have been eating junk in front of the television.

It was during a forty day fast that Moses received the 10 Commandments. So many big things happened in the Bible just after or during a fast. I will be discussing a number of them in this section of this book. Fasting definitely brings change.

> "And the Lord said unto Moses, Write thou these words: for after the tenor of these words I have made a covenant with thee and with Israel.
>
> And he was there with the Lord forty days and forty nights; he did neither eat bread, nor drink water. And he wrote upon the tables the words of the covenant, the ten commandments." Exodus 34:27-28

There will not be awesome and miraculous things happening every single day of your fast. There are going to be days when it is extremely difficult and you just do not want to do it. There are going to be days when cheeseburgers are calling out your name loudly! Be prepared for that and ride it out.

Another time the Bible mentions a corporate fast is when Haman ordered the horrible treatment and murder of all the Jews. Esther called for every Jew in her city to fast with her for 3 days. The fast was called and afterward the Jews were spared! This account is in Esther chapters 4 to 7.

When Hannah was greatly hurting because she was barren, she did not eat (fasted) and spent time in the house of the Lord.

> *"And as he did so year by year, when she went up to the house of the Lord, so she provoked her; therefore she wept, and did not eat." 1 Samuel 1:7*

She fasted and then conceived and gave birth to Samuel. In the Bible you can also read that Daniel did a 21 day partial fast, Joshua fasted for 40 days and that the Apostle Paul fasted at least twice that is recorded in the Bible.

CHAPTER 11: THREE CATEGORIES OF FASTING

MEDICAL DISCLAIMER: DO NOT ENTER ANY TYPE OF FAST WITHOUT APPROVAL FROM YOUR DOCTOR.

The fast that is most common and normal is the fast were you go with out food for a sum of days but you take in liquids. Then there is the Daniel fast (also known as a partial fast) where you eat only fruits and vegetables along with liquids. You need to know what the Lord is saying for you to do and be clear about the spiritual purpose of your fast.

There is scientific evidence that fasting is good for riding your body of toxins. Your breath can get really bad as your body is cleansing, so keep washed and teeth brushed! Participating in a fast means that you are doing something for your spiritual strength, and you receive the side benefit of doing something also for your physical strength. What you give up during your fast needs to mean something to you. For example, if you hate orange juice, then giving up orange juice will not be appropriate. In that instance, giving up orange juice would not be considered a huge sacrifice in the eyes of God!

Let your children see that Jehovah God is most important and is worthy of our time and attention. What Christian walk are you modeling in front of your children? Do they ever hear you praying fervently out loud? Do they see seeking God as a normal part of a believer's life?

> *"I beseech you therefore, brethren, by the mercies of God, that ye present your bodies a living sacrifice, holy, acceptable unto God, which is your reasonable service." Romans 12:1*

In Romans 12:1 we are out-right told to present out bodies as a living sacrifice. Praying and fasting are two ways things are acceptable to God and is your reasonable service

When Daniel fasted it was because he was grieved over what was happening to Israel. Daniel really sought God in prayer during his fast. After the fast ended in Daniel chapter 10, an angel came! We see that his fast directly resulted in some angelic visitation.

In Acts chapter 9:7 – 9 we have an example of fasting. Saul was on the road to Damascus when the Lord stopped and met with Him. He did not eat or drink immediately following this encounter. It was during a fast God revealed to him the mandate and calling that was on his life.

> *"The men traveling with Saul stood there speechless; they heard the sound but did not see anyone. Saul got up from the ground, but when he opened his eyes he could see nothing. So they led him by the hand into Damascus. For three days he was blind, and did not eat or drink anything." Acts 9:7-9*

I fail to see how we would be able to walk in the center of God's will without getting direction during times of prayer and fasting. We need our spiritual ears open so we can hear Him and then obey what He is saying. We were created to hear His voice.

"My sheep hear my voice, and I know them, and they follow me." John 10:27 King James Version

The Lord Almighty speaks and we can hear and discern what He is saying! He is the one with all the wisdom and all the answers and He is willing to speak! Therefore, I quiet myself, tune everything else out, and let Him talk.

"And afterward,I will pour out my Spirit on all people. Your sons and daughters will prophesy, your old men will dream dreams, your young men will see visions." Joel 2:28 New International Version

The Word of God says that He wants to pour out revival "afterward". So, the question is after what? The answer is: after a fast. Just a few verses above in Joel 2:15 we read that a fast was called.

"Blow the trumpet in Zion, declare a holy fast, call a sacred assembly. " Joel 2:15 New International Version

There is a promise in the Bible that when you will pray and seek God's face, He will heal. If believers really took a hold of this and humbled themselves (which I totally interpret to include fasting) and prayed there would be a bunch more healing in this land. The church just needs to get revelation and call a time of corporate fasting and prayer.

"If my people, which are called by my name, shall humble themselves, and pray, and seek my face, and turn from their wicked ways; then will I hear from heaven, and will forgive their sin, and will heal their land." 2 Chronicles 7:14 King James Version

Now I will take you to 2 Chronicle 20: 3 -17 where Jehosophat found himself completely desperate. He was surrounded by the enemy's strong army. Jehosophat responded by calling a corporate fast. He had all of Judah (including the woman and children) fast so they would get divine strategy to defeat the bigger (in the natural) enemy army. He went before the people fasting and started to worship God. Read the supernatural result of that fast in 2 Chronicles 20: 3 – 17.

> *"And Jehoshaphat feared, and set himself to seek the Lord, and proclaimed a fast throughout all Judah. And Judah gathered themselves together, to ask help of the Lord: even out of all the cities of Judah they came to seek the Lord. And Jehoshaphat stood in the congregation of Judah and Jerusalem, in the house of the Lord, before the new court,*
>
> *And said, O Lord God of our fathers, art not thou God in heaven? and rulest not thou over all the kingdoms of the heathen? and in thine hand is there not power and might, so that none is able to withstand thee? Art not thou our God, who didst drive out the inhabitants of this land before thy people Israel, and gavest it to the seed of Abraham thy friend for ever? And they dwelt therein, and have built thee a sanctuary therein for thy name, saying, If, when evil cometh upon us, as the sword, judgment, or pestilence, or famine, we stand before this house, and in thy presence, (for thy name is in this house,) and cry unto thee in our affliction, then thou wilt hear and help. And now, behold, the children of Ammon and Moab and mount Seir, whom thou wouldest not let Israel invade, when they came out of the land of Egypt, but they turned from them, and destroyed them not; Behold, I say, how they reward us, to come to cast us out of thy possession,*

which thou hast given us to inherit. O our God, wilt thou not judge them? for we have no might against this great company that cometh against us; neither know we what to do: but our eyes are upon thee.

And all Judah stood before the Lord, with their little ones, their wives, and their children. Then upon Jahaziel the son of Zechariah, the son of Benaiah, the son of Jeiel, the son of Mattaniah, a Levite of the sons of Asaph, came the Spirit of the Lord in the midst of the congregation;

And he said, Hearken ye, all Judah, and ye inhabitants of Jerusalem, and thou king Jehoshaphat, Thus saith the Lord unto you, Be not afraid nor dismayed by reason of this great multitude; for the battle is not yours, but God's. To morrow go ye down against them: behold, they come up by the cliff of Ziz; and ye shall find them at the end of the brook, before the wilderness of Jeruel. Ye shall not need to fight in this battle: set yourselves, stand ye still, and see the salvation of the Lord with you, O Judah and Jerusalem: fear not, nor be dismayed; to morrow go out against them: for the Lord will be with you." 2 Chronicles 20:3-17

They put their eyes on the Lord and the answer came! They sought the Lord and then heard from the Lord! (*2 Chronicles 20:12: "we do not know what to do, but our eyes are on You."*) God told them in detail how that enemy army would approach. He also explained to them exactly what they were to do in response. They had themselves a time of worship and praise after that! They obeyed and won. The Lord ambushed the enemy and the enemy was defeated. Do you want God to tell you what you need to do at this time in your life? If the answer is yes, then fast, worship, and seek Him. Jehosophat did not whine in a time of great distress or stay in bed with the covers over his head. He did not give up and do nothing. He would not allow himself to be filled with the thinking it was all over. No! He called a corporate time of prayer and fasting. God prospered them and delivered them out of the hand of the enemy. Almighty God is willing to show you His plan to have all the plans of the enemy thwarted in your life.

The wisdom of the Lord is being spoken to you, but you have to put yourself in position to hear. To hear it you must forsake other things to pursue tuning in to Him.

Praise and fasting pushes back the enemy. During times of fasting you will probably find that even worship can get to a whole new level!

Satan gets anxious and annoyed when you decide to be more than a sleepy, pew-warming Christian. The devil knows that fasting releases God's power. Resist temptation. Resist the devil's plans to get you off track and off focus.

When you are on a juice fast, friends will come out of the woodwork and invite you to lunch! Not only does the enemy try to de-rail you, but well-meaning and loving friends may call and want to go for a meal. On top of that, they may even offer to pay! I was on a fast one time and people I rarely see wanted to take me for lunch.

When Satan tempted Jesus to turn the stone into bread Jesus refused to fall for that trick. Jesus could have turned that stone into bread, but He didn't. He was determined to finish the fast God had called Him to do. When Jesus finished that forty day fast, immediately he began to do mighty miracles.

I have read an account of an ex-Satanist who shared with a group of believers that Satanists fast and pray to gain more power from the devil. This man also mentioned that Christians have a reputation amongst some Satanists of being people of little prayer and fasting.

The devil tries so hard to keep us distracted. Are you going to focus on your appetite as well as the circumstances that surround you? Have your focus solely on the promises of God that will be released when you employ the powerful weapon of fasting?

CHAPTER 12:

REWARDS OF GOD

"But without faith it is impossible to please him: for he that cometh to God must believe that he is, and that he is a rewarder of them that diligently seek him." Hebrews 11:6 King James Version

God truly rewards those that diligently seek Him (Hebrews 11:6). The rewards that God has for those that diligently seek Him are simply waiting to be released upon those whose focus is Him. You will get addicted to hanging out with God! Nothing else will satisfy and the rewards will be amazing.

If we neglect to do what it takes to stay sharp and sensitive to the Holy Spirit, our praise, worship, offerings and even our preaching can become routine and void of anointing. Jehovah God is not happy with our leftovers, but leftovers are what we often hand Him. We are running around doing all sorts of other things (even church things) that we barely speak to the One who should mean the most to us.

When you put God first, He becomes willing to reveal to you things that He keeps hidden from lazy, casual, and lukewarm Christians. One powerful way you can seek the Lord is through prayer and fasting.

"I SOUGHT the Lord, and He heard me, and delivered me from all my fears." Psalms 34:4 King James Version

The best, most advantageous thing you can do when you need a breakthrough is not to whine, complain nor get discouraged, but to worship God with all you have got. Keep your eyes locked onto His face and His Word. Magnify Him. Put a magnifying glass up to our already enormous God and focus on nothing else.

Magnify and praise God. We read in 2 Chronicles chapter 20 that Jehosophat sent the singers in ahead of the army to magnify and praise the Lord. We know that attitude of worship during a difficult time brought divine intervention.

" Yet a time is coming and has now come when the true worshipers will worship the Father in the Spirit and in truth, for they are the kind of worshipers the Father seeks." John 4:23 New International Version

"But he said to them, "I have food to eat that you know nothing about."

Then his disciples said to each other, "Could someone have brought him food?"

"My food," said Jesus, "is to do the will of him who sent me and to finish his work." John 4:32-34 New International Version

There are people who are so cautious and diligent about what food they put into their bodies. They work out and do not want to gain weight or become unhealthy. I am all for being disciplined in eating and exercising. Live a long, strong life so you can preach the gospel. But, what is your spirit feeding on? We need to be even more aware and cautious of our spiritual health and growth.

Is your spirit growing and getting a work out? Are we taking the same effort with our spiritual health?

> *"Jesus answered, "It is written: 'Man shall not live on bread alone, but on every word that comes from the mouth of God.'" Matthew 4:4 New International Version*

Are you a malnourished Christian? If you have read this far in this book, then I believe you are one that does not want to play church. Your desire is to be the church. People who are hungry for more of God are desperate people. Truly desperate people do what is necessary and make changes. Let your praises and worship to Him be born out of a longing to be with Him and not out of some route, religious exercise that has lost all intensity.

Here is the account in Acts 10:4 of Cornelius. Cornelius was a man of prayer. As he was praying one day an angel appeared to him with a message. I don't know about you, but I always enjoy messages from the Lord.

> *"There was a certain man in Caesarea called Cornelius, a centurion of the band called the Italian band, A devout man, and one that feared God with all his house, which gave much alms to the people, and prayed to God always. He saw in a vision evidently about the ninth hour of the day an angel of God coming in to him, and saying unto him, Cornelius. And when he looked on him, he was afraid, and said,What is it, Lord? And he said unto him, Thy prayers and thine alms are come up for a memorial before God. And now send men to Joppa, and call for one Simon, whose surname is Peter: He lodgeth with one Simon a tanner, whose house is by the sea side: he shall tell thee what thou oughtest to*

do. And when the angel which spake unto Cornelius was departed, he called two of his household servants, and a devout soldier of them that waited on him continually; And when he had declared all these things unto them, he sent them to Joppa. On the morrow, as they went on their journey, and drew nigh unto the city, Peter went up upon the housetop to pray about the sixth hour: And he became very hungry, and would have eaten: but while they made ready, he fell into a trance," Acts 10:1-10 King James Version

The purpose of fasting and prayer is not to manipulate God. Rather, it is a tool that puts you in a place to hear Him and therefore be highly effective during these end-times days. In Acts 10, Cornelius knew God, but he didn't know Jesus as Messiah. The Bible describes Cornelius as one who was devoted to God. This means that God was Cornelius' priority. An angel appeared to Cornelius and told him to send for Peter in Joppa. Then the angel included that he should heed what Peter was about to say. Cornelius was not sitting at home, spending loads of time on activities that do not affect eternity. He wasn't completely ignoring God when this angel came and spoke to him but the Bible says he prayed to God always. One of the rewards for those that diligently seek Him is divine direction. When Peter arrived at his house, Cornelius said

"Four days ago I was fasting until this hour; and at the ninth hour I prayed in my house, and behold, a man stood before me in bright clothing, and said, "Cornelius, your prayer has been heard, and your alms have been remembered in the sight of God." King James Version

Cornelius was seeking the Lord with fasting and prayer when he received this divine encounter with Peter.

> *"Blow the trumpet in Zion, declare a holy fast, call a sacred assembly. Gather the people, consecrate the assembly; bring together the elders, gather the children, those nursing at the breast. Let the bridegroom leave his room and the bride her chamber."*
> *Joel 2:15-16 New International Version*

In Joel 2 the people were so poor and in such a famine that they were trying to come up with an offering for the Lord. God told them to blow the trumpet in Zion, sanctify a fast, and call a solemn assembly. Even the women, elders, and children were included. After the fast the threshing floor was full of wheat, the oil vats were overflowing! They ate in plenty and were satisfied. Now that is fasting for a breakthrough!

> *"Be glad then, ye children of Zion, and rejoice in the Lord your God: for he hath given you the former rain moderately, and he will cause to come down for you the rain, the former rain, and the latter rain in the first month. And the floors shall be full of wheat, and the vats shall overflow with wine and oil. And I will restore to you the years that the locust hath eaten, the cankerworm, and the caterpillar, and the palmerworm, my great army which I sent among you. And ye shall eat in plenty, and be satisfied, and praise the name of the Lord your God, that hath dealt wondrously with you: and my people shall never be ashamed. And ye shall know that I am in the midst of Israel, and that I am the Lord your God, and none else: and my people shall never be ashamed." Joel 2: 23-27 King James Version*

Isaiah 58:6-9 is another scripture on the exciting benefits of fasting.

> "Is not this the fast that I have chosen? to loose the bands of wickedness, to undo the heavy burdens, and to let the oppressed go free, and that ye break every yoke? Is it not to deal thy bread to the hungry, and that thou bring the poor that are cast out to thy house? when thou seest the naked, that thou cover him; and that thou hide not thyself from thine own flesh? Then shall thy light break forth as the morning, and thine health shall spring forth speedily: and thy righteousness shall go before thee; the glory of the Lord shall be thy reward. Then shalt thou call, and the Lord shall answer; thou shalt cry, and he shall say, Here I am. If thou take away from the midst of thee the yoke, the putting forth of the finger, and speaking vanity" Isaiah 58:6-9 King James Version

There are churches crying out to God for members of their congregation to be healed. There are churches that each week invite people that are in need of healing come to the front for some prayer. We need to add fasting to that equation for some real power. We just read fasting being linked to healing springing forth and the glory of the Lord coming and protecting.

> Let's always consider *Matthew 17:21 [But this kind does not go out except by prayer and fasting."]* New American Standard Version.

I didn't write the Bible. I'm just telling you what it says. Sometimes the answers we are looking for requires us to do something! Instead of continually crying out for God to do something, look into the Word and see what our part of the equation is. Is God waiting on you? Victory happens when you take action in obedience to the Word of God.

In Judges chapter 19 and 20, the armies of the Israel gathered against Benjamin. 22,000 men were lost on the first day of the battle. (Judges 20:21).

The next day they fought against the Benjamites again, this time losing 18,000 (verse 25). God sent the prophet Phineahs to them before the battle on the third day. The prophet had a message for them to fast and pray and once they did, demonic strongholds started to break off.

CHAPTER 13: OUTPOURING AFTER A FAST

Remember we are told in Matthew 6:4 that Father God will Himself reward you openly. You can take it to the bank that God does not lie. Churches that have corporate fasts can expect an increase in souls. In fact, fasting will take every aspect of your life to the next level. He wants to bless you and show the world that He takes note of those that are dedicated to obeying Him.

Fasting makes you more sensitive to the timing and voice of the Holy Spirit. Fasting will help fine tune your spirit to know the order and wisdom of God. He is so willing to speak to you. He will share answers! Can you hear His leading?

There are things that you may already know that God wants you to do. Fasting will release to you the steps, details, resources and anointing to carry out His will for you on this earth.

Jesus understands the difficulty of depriving ourselves of food. He himself fasted while He was on earth in human form. Tap into His strength and anointing. Get lost in Him because He will enable you to do all things.

> *"For we do not have a high priest who cannot sym-*
> *pathize with our weaknesses, but One who has been*

tempted in all things as we are, yet without sin."
Hebrews 4:15 New American Standard Bible

I love using a concordance to study a subject. The next mention of fasting is the elderly prophetess named Anna. She was often in the temple and she fasted.

> *And she was a widow of about fourscore and four*
> *years, which departed not from the temple, but*
> *served God with fastings and prayers night and day.*
> *And she coming in that instant gave thanks likewise*
> *unto the Lord, and spake of him to all them that*
> *looked for redemption in Jerusalem. Luke 2:37-38*
> *King James Version (KJV)*

It was because of fasting that she knew when the Messiah came into the temple to be dedicated. In Bible commentaries, it is mentioned the likelihood that the temple was extremely busy with quite the crowds when Joseph and Mary brought Jesus to be dedicated. Out of all those people at the temple at that time, there were only two that knew that child was the Messiah. Simeon and Anna sought the Lord and heard His voice. Fasting tuned in Anna's spirit to recognize the Son of God. She knew it was Him when He came into the temple when many others did not. Prayer will illuminate blockages to receiving the promises of God and during prayer the instructions to eliminate those blockages will be received. There are plenty of promises regarding prosperity in the Word of God that hinge on us doing something. There is also a principle behind every promise that needs to be learned and applied. Fasting with unhindered prayer and Bible reading brings great revelation to these principles and questions get answered.

Faith comes from hearing and hearing and hearing. I does not come from one time hearing the anointed preaching of the Word in the past. Faith does not come from "heard" and does

NOT come from anything other than the Word. Make sure you are speaking scriptures to people! Too many Christians find themselves spiritually malnourished because they do not have the Word a priority. Those people will not live a life pleasing God. Faith comes from hearing the WORD and without faith it is impossible to please God. Always honour the Word of God as first place and final authority.

> *"But he answered and said, It is written, Man shall not live by bread alone, but by every word that proceedeth out of the mouth of God." Matthew 4:4 King James Version*

You can't just live by natural food. I will mention again how vitally important is it to also take care of your spiritual life

> *"Heaven and earth shall pass away: but my words shall not pass away." Mark 13:31 King James Version*

During the first day of your fast you might not receive massive miracles nor your complete breakthrough. That is why some fasts are 40 days. Do not be discouraged because you might not get thrust into full time ministry the first or second day of your fast.

In Acts chapter one, the believers needed to be patient in the Upper Room. They were given the instruction to tarry. I was shocked to read and note how many people grew impatient and left. It started out with quite a few people and ended up with a small amount of people that would obey. The were asked to wait upon the Lord for however long it took. To wait (or tarry) is completely a matter of discipline over our flesh. Fasting as part of your Christian walk helps you be willing to be disciplined. The flesh does not like waiting for breakthrough as we prefer instant gratification. Do not give in to discouragement. Wait upon the Lord by being a **wait**or/**wait**ress and serve Him with joy. Tarry so you do not miss out on upper room type of experiences.

Jesus said that we would do even greater works! Really, truly let that sink in as you meditate on John 14:12.

> *"Verily, verily, I say unto you, He that believeth on me, the works that I do shall he do also; and greater works than these shall he do; because I go unto my Father." John 14:12 King James Version*

Are you doing greater things, or even great things? I am never going to say that I have no further to grow. We all have room to grow so we can do greater and greater things! Remember that as long as there is one unsaved person on the earth, there work for us to do. I want to stay on the cutting edge of what God is doing and thinking. I want to get to heaven and hear Him say, *"Well done."* Do you think some people will hear, "You have *not done* much."? Faith without works is dead. We are expected to fulfil the mandate and commission of the church to preach the gospel to every person. Fasting increases boldness factor for witnessing as well as willingness to do whatever He asks.

Fasting and getting close to God is for freedom. It releases authority for mountains to be moved. You can cry and complain all you want. You can beg God to do something, but He has done everything He is going to do in most cases. He is waiting on us to do our part. He's waiting for us to fast and pray and pull down some strongholds. Are we sitting on the couch watching television, waiting for some miracle to drop on our laps? Go! Speak to the mountains. God isn't going to do if for you. You have to say to the mountain, "be removed." Read that verse and it shows you that there are some things that God isn't going to do for you. You need to open your mouth.

"And Jesus answered and said unto them, Verily I say unto you, If ye have faith, and doubt not, ye shall not only do what is done to the fig tree, but even if ye shall say unto this mountain, Be thou taken up and cast into the sea, it shall be done." Matthew 17:20 New American Standard Bible

Can you discern the difference between your thoughts and God's thoughts? Fasting is one way to turn up the volume on the God channel! There is no higher authority than to know the heart of God in the situation you are facing. If you need a word from God, are you willing to do whatever it takes to hear from Him?

In Exodus 13:11-12 God makes it clear that the firstlings of flocks, first fruits of harvest, firstborn of males in families, and all other firsts belong to Him. He wants to not get the leftovers of our time.

Western Church is sometimes very self-focused. We can be "all about me." Sometimes the only thing we give God is not our reasonable service, but instead only our list of things that we want. While those are legitimate needs and desires, we must remember Matthew 6:33 tells us that if God is our priority, all "things" will be added unto us.

"He must increase, but I must decrease." John 3:30 New American Standard Bible

Our thoughts need to be consumed with His wants, which I believe is souls. As we are busy with His business, He takes care of our business.

Romans 8:13 is a verse that fits with the topic of putting God first.

"For if you live according to the flesh, you will die; but if by the Spirit you put to death the deeds of the body, you will live." Romans 8:13 King James Version

You would think that the numbers of Christians would be growing by huge leaps and bounds. We have 24/7 Christian television programming, a massive number of Christian books and internet web sites that will give you Bible helps. Add to that the abundance of churches along with the freedom to worship…. Yet sin is what is growing rapidly in North America. Believers must grow in boldness and moving in divine strategy downloaded from Heaven to get the waiting harvest in! We need to stay spiritually alert because our enemy prowls around wanting to devour us. Head principalities over areas are very real. So why are we spending such little time in prayer to hear the Lord and pull down the strongholds? In North America, I have met countless Christians who are very close to ignoring God, just to blame Him when the enemy gets a stronghold.

"Do not be deceived: God cannot be mocked. A man reaps what he sows. Whoever sows to please their flesh, from the flesh will reap destruction; whoever sows to please the Spirit, from the Spirit will reap eternal life." Galatians 6:7-8 New International Version

We need to be effective and adept at wielding that Sword known as the Bible in application. Does the Word of God have first place in your life?

The Scripture that is rightly divided is a powerful weapon with a razor-sharp edge that slashes demons when you speak! This weapon that we all have need of should not sit on the shelf and collect dust. We can have this weapon and never get familiar enough with it to even know where the trigger is.

I love listening to preachers and have grown much from them. However, I always take what they say and search it out in scriptures. You can not own for yourself and give out to others what you don't understand.

> *"In the beginning was the Word, and the Word was with God, and the Word was God." John 1:1 King James Version*

The Word is God (John 1:1). How you treat The Word is how you treat God! Reading the Bible during a fast is a must.

I have had pastors tell me that they would lose congregation members if they asked people to fast. They claim that people do not want to hear about fasting so they never preach nor teach on that subject. They same pastors wonder why breakthroughs are not more abundant!

We are here to please God and not people. Preachers should not just say what will tickle your ears. Preachers need to speak what will erase your excuses and challenge you to grow.

In Jonah 3 we read where God sent Jonah to preach repentance to Nineveh. God had such mercy and spared the city of Nineveh. The people of Nineveh began to seek God again. However, it was not long after that when the prophet Nahum prophesied judgement over that city in Nahum 1:4. They went back to their old ways! Don't get on fire and then lose it. Don't be all excited about God because you went to the best conference and then a week later you are "back to normal." Did God save you and spare you from hell and that no longer excites you? Okay, I'll get back to the topic of fasting, but it is all part of a bigger, maturity (milk to meat) picture.

Don't confer with flesh regarding spiritual matters. Don't ask someone who is not saved about spiritual matters. Flesh is not going to give you spiritual answers. Find people that cause you to grow greatly in the Lord. And, when they are not available or they get off track, you need to yourself encouraged in the Lord.

> "And David was greatly distressed; for the people spake of stoning him, because the soul of all the people was grieved, every man for his sons and for his daughters: but David encouraged himself in the Lord his God." 1 Samuel 30:6 King James Version

I am specific in my reason for fasting. I have clear purpose. Habakkuk 2:2 tells us to write the vision and make it plain. Making it plain means you can lock onto what God is doing and because of the clarity you will not get easily side-tracked. I use that scripture in teaching on finances and also in my teaching on vision. Know what it is you are fasting for, then get ready for a whole lot more revelation that you even realized you needed! God's wisdom is always getting downloaded to those who are seriously, diligently, wanting answers.

Going back to Isaiah 58:10-12

> "and if you spend yourselves in behalf of the hungry and satisfy the needs of the oppressed, then your light will rise in the darkness, and your night will become like the noonday. The Lord will guide you always; He will satisfy your needs in a sun-scorched land and will strengthen your frame. You will be like a well-watered garden, like a spring whose waters never fail. Your people will rebuild the ancient ruins and will raise up the age-old foundations; you will be called Repairer of Broken Walls, Restorer of

Streets with Dwellings." Isaiah 58:10-12 New International Version

When you have a major decision to make, wouldn't you like to know what way to turn? When you need some direction, wouldn't you like Jehovah God to illuminate the path that you are to take? He knows everything, so be quiet and let Him talk. Wisdom will come to you! You will have the answers you need! You will be guided by the Lord. Your ears will be tuned into the God channel and you will hear Isaiah 58:12 *"This is the way, walk in it."* You need to discipline your flesh to take a back seat.

> *"And Joshua said unto the people, Sanctify your-selves: for tomorrow the Lord will do wonders among you." James 3:5 King James Version*

What are you doing to sanctify yourself? Sanctify yourself today and the Lord will show up and do wonders among you tomorrow. This is exciting stuff. It is showing that we have to do our part.

> *"For I am the Lord your God: ye shall therefore sanctify yourselves, and ye shall be holy; for I am holy: neither shall ye defile yourselves with any manner of creeping thing that creepeth upon the earth." Leviticus 11:44 King James Version*

Sanctifying and consecrating ourselves means putting off and putting away the things of the world and taking on the Word. I thought that I was living a pretty clean, holy life until I started fasting and realized what things He still wanted purged. It brought me to a whole new level of understanding regarding what is acceptable to God. There is no condemnation, but precious conviction and correction so we do not live below what God has available for us.

"Take heed, brethren, lest there be in any of you an evil heart of unbelief, in departing from the living God. But exhort one another daily, while it is called To day; lest any of you be hardened through the deceitfulness of sin. For we are made partakers of Christ, if we hold the beginning of our confidence stedfast unto the end; " Hebrews 3:12-14 King James Version

Fasting showed me areas of unbelief that before fasting I had not seen as unbelief. In Hebrews chapter 3 God calls unbelief "wicked" or "evil". We should want to be purged from what God considers evil.

Fast, sanctify yourself, and put Him Lord over everything.

Section Three:
Receiving Healing

CHAPTER 14: WORD OF GOD ONLY. NOT CIRCUMSTANCES

John 14: 12 -14 "Very truly I tell you, whoever believes in me will do the works I have been doing, and they will do even greater things than these, because I am going to the Father. And I will do whatever you ask in my name, so that the Father may be glorified in the Son. You may ask me for anything in my name, and I will do it." New International Version

You are about to embark on a wonderful journey of living a lifestyle of *"greater things"* (John 14:12). Let us start by exploring what the Bible, from Genesis to Revelation, says about healing. The Bible is our final authority, not our previous experiences or symptoms. Theology comes from the Word of God alone and not from perceived failures. Jump into the Word and meditate on what the Word says about healing. *I will start in the Old Testament and carry on into the New Testament using different Bible versions and in an almost point-form format. Don't expect it this section to read like a novel.* In addition, ask the Holy Spirit for further revelation on what you are reading and then sit down and buckle-up!

"And said, If thou wilt diligently hearken to the voice of the Lord thy God, and wilt do that which is

> *right in his sight, and wilt give ear to his command-*
> *ments, and keep all his statutes, I will put none of*
> *these diseases upon thee, which I have brought upon*
> *the Egyptians: for I am the Lord that healeth thee."*
> Exodus 15:26 King James Version

The Lord heals! He does not make you sick. He is your healer!

Exodus 23: 25-26 does not say that He is the Lord that puts sickness on you.

> *"And ye shall serve the Lord your God, and he shall*
> *bless thy bread, and thy water; and I will take sick-*
> *ness away from the midst of thee. There shall nothing*
> *cast their young, nor be barren, in thy land: the*
> *number of thy days I will fulfil."* Exodus 23:25-26

His will is that those that serve Him would have a healthy, long, full life. You do not have to wonder what the will of God is. Anything other than good health is not from God.

Deuteronomy 28: look at the following verses (there is so much in there that I will just do the highlights). The number on the left represents the verse in Deuteronomy 28.

1. the Lord God will exalt you above the nations.

2. You will experience all the blessings if (there is a condition) you obey.

3. You will be blessed is mentioned numerous times! (He wants you to receive that since it is mentioned more than once).

4. The Lord will conquer your enemies.

5. The Lord will bless everything you do and your storehouses will be full.
   (Storehouses are only needed when the house is full).

6. The nations of the world will see that God's people are blessed and will stand in awe!! God wants to show off that He is good.

7. The Lord will give you an abundance of good things.

Read Deuteronomy 28 and get revelation of God's heart towards the righteous. The word "blessed" is mentioned numerous times in Deuteronomy 28 and it means "happy and to be envied." People are not going to be envied when they are sick!

According to the rest of Deuteronomy 28, illness is part of the curse and we do not have to live under the curse.

God wants people (nations) to look upon the righteous with awe and envy because of the abundance (and not shortage) of good things. I do not consider health problems or financial lack *"an abundance of good things"* as stated in Deuteronomy 28:7

Where does it say in scripture that God gets glory when we are sick or diseased?

Persecution or suffering for preaching the gospel is different than what we are talking about here. Going to jail for preaching the gospel is not an infirmity and not the subject of this teaching. We are never told to endure an infirmity, but we are told that there will be persecution for preaching the gospel.

> *"See, I have set before thee this day life and good, and death and evil; " Deuteronomy 30:15 King James Version*

Deuteronomy 30:15 tells us that we are given a choice between prosperity or disaster, between life and death. Is the choice up to God? God is sovereign and He decided that to make the choice up to us. Your life is not in the devil's hands, it is in your mouth. Every day we have the choice of whether we want to choose God's way or the devil's way. Your life goes the way your mouth goes. Look at Proverbs 18:21 and see that life and death are in your tongue.

> "Death and life are in the power of the tongue: and they that love it shall eat the fruit thereof." Proverbs 18:21 King James Version

In Genesis, God created the heavens and the earth by speaking. We are made in His image which means that what comes out of our mouth will be created. In Hebrew the word for "words" is debar and the word for "things" is also debar. We have to watch what we say because there is such a close relation to what we say to what we have.

> "Many are the afflictions of the righteous: but the Lord delivereth him out of them all." Psalms 34:19 King James Version

> "There shall no evil befall thee, neither shall any plague come nigh thy dwelling." Psalms 91:10 King James Version

That sounds like a God who doesn't want His children in physical pain. Psalm 91 talks about supernatural protection from harm which includes plagues.

> "For he shall give his angels charge over thee, to keep thee in all thy ways. They shall bear thee up in their hands, lest thou dash thy foot against a stone. Thou shalt tread upon the lion and adder: the young lion

and the dragon shalt thou trample under feet."
Psalms 91:11-13 King James Version

He orders His angels to protect you wherever you go. They will hold you with their hands to keep you from striking your foot on a stone. If God will send angels so we don't even hurt our foot, why would He want any other part of our body sore or not working?

I have not read one scripture that refers to cancer as something God would use to teach us something. The Bible says that the word was sent for our correction. It does not say that illness was sent for our correction.

> *"All scripture is given by inspiration of God, and is profitable for doctrine, for reproof, for correction, for instruction in righteousness" 2 Timothy 3:16 King James Version*

You wouldn't place someone behind your car and back over them to teach them a lesson. Someone who did that would end up in jail. Do we honestly think that the nature and character of God is like one of those people? I have learned to be very careful and mindful of what I say about the nature, character and integrity of God. He provided healing and it is an insult to His character to say He put it on you.

> *"With long life I will satisfy him and show him my salvation." Psalms 91:16 New International Version*

The word "salvation" means more than just entrance into Heaven. In Hebrew it means: deliverance, aid, victory, prosperity, and health. That doesn't sound like our God wants us sick or broke. We may choose sick and broke, but that is not His desire for us. You don't need to guess what the will of God is for your life. It is clearly spelled out in His Word.

We are NOT the sick trying to get healed. We are the healed, blood-bought saints. The devil is trying to have us accept an illness.

> *"Praise the Lord, my soul, and forget not all his benefits" Psalms 103:2 New International Version*

Long life and complete healing while on earth are parts of the benefits. We are instructed not to forget that or you will live below God's will for you.

> *"For the Lord God is a sun and shield; the Lord bestows favor and honor; no good thing does he withhold from those whose walk is blameless."* Psalms 84:11 New International Version

No good thing (including healing) will God withhold. So, if something good is being withheld, it's not God doing that. Our mouth is likely what the blessing blocker is.

> *"Who satisfies your years with good things, So that your youth is renewed like the eagle." Psalms 103:5 New American Standard Bible*

Illness is not a good thing! Since He satisfies you with good things, He did not give any illness to you. I do not know of anyone who would view physical pain and a bad doctor report as a good thing.

> *"He brought them forth also with silver and gold: and there was not one feeble person among their tribes." Psalms 105:37 King James Version*

Theologians estimate Moses led possibly 2,000.000 people and not one of them were sick or feeble. God's will and desire for His people is that there would be no feeble among us.

"My son, give attention to my words; Incline your ear to my sayings. Do not let them depart from your sight; Keep them in the midst of your heart. For they are life to those who find them and health to all their body." Proverbs 4:20-22 New American Standard Version

Listen to the Lord and have health in your body! God's will is for health. Does that sound too good to be true? It's not! The medicine in the Word of God available to you every moment of every day with no side effects!

"Watch over your heart with all diligence, For from it flow the springs of life. Put away from you a deceitful mouth And put devious speech far from you." Proverbs 4:23-24 New American Standard Bible

Give your attention to the Bible. Guard your heart! Watch your mouth. Keep heart and mouth lined up with the Word. Set your heart on His Word and enjoy good health! Inclining your ear is so much more than just showing up in church and warming a pew. You need to receive, believe and apply the Word that you are hearing.

"The one who guards his mouth preserves his life; The one who opens wide his lips comes to ruin." Proverbs 13:3 New American Standard Bible

CHAPTER 15 WHAT DOES YOUR TONGUE SAY?

My tongue says that I am healed and I am whole. My words line up with the Word of God and nothing else. If you guard your heart and mouth to only speak the Word, you will eventually have your circumstances come into line with the Word. Stay consistent and do not give up. Take back what the devil has stolen. I don't want anything in my health or life to be missing or broken.

> " My people are destroyed for lack of knowledge. Because you have rejected knowledge, I also will reject you from being My priest. Since you have forgotten the law of your God, I also will forget your children." Hosea 4:6 New American Standard Bible

"My people" means us believers. We are His people. We are being destroyed for lack of revelation knowledge of what our rights are according to the Word of God. (I mentioned this in section one of this book regarding finances). We are destroyed not for lack of money or health coverage, but lack of knowledge. If you don't have revelation knowledge regarding your covenant with God, then you will live below your rights and life in defeat (destroyed).

> "Do you not know? Have you not heard? The Lord is the everlasting God, the Creator of the

ends of the earth. He will not grow tired or weary, and his understanding no one can fathom. He gives strength to the weary and increases the power of the weak. Even youths grow tired and weary, and young men stumble and fall; but those who hope in the Lord will renew their strength. They will soar on wings like eagles; they will run and not grow weary, they will walk and not be faint." Isaiah 40:28-31 New International Version

His will is for us to receive the power and strength that He offers. To "wait upon the Lord" does not mean that you do nothing. A waiter or waitress waits on a table with gladness (as mentioned earlier). He or she serves with joy and receives benefit (pay and tips) from doing so. Wait on the Lord by serving Him with gladness and see your youth be renewed!

"Surely he hath borne our griefs, and carried our sorrows: yet we did esteem him stricken, smitten of God, and afflicted.

But he was wounded for our transgressions, he was bruised for our iniquities: the chastisement of our peace was upon him; and with his stripes we are healed." Isaiah 53:4-5 King James Version

Isaiah was speaking prophetically about the results of the cross in Isaiah chapter 53. In the New Testament gospels, we read the physical account of what happened at the cross, but Isaiah is seeing the spiritual results of the cross.

He was wounded with 39 lashes. Every disease that has been discovered (and that could be in the thousands) can be placed into 39 categories. We are healed!

> *" Yet it was the Lord's will to crush him and cause him to suffer, and though the Lord makes his life an offering for sin, he will see his offspring and prolong his days, and the will of the Lord will prosper in his hand." Isaiah 53:10 New International Version*

Isaiah 53 states clearly and plainly that it was the will of the Lord to bruise Him. It was the will of God to put the sickness on Jesus and make Him carry our sickness. Then how could it be the will of God to make us carry those same sicknesses? That would be like having Jesus carry them for nothing.

> *"Have you not put a hedge around him and his household and everything he has? You have blessed the work of his hands, so that his flocks and herds are spread throughout the land." Job 1:10 New International Version*

I think Satan had to ask if there was a hedge because Satan could not see a hedge. If there was a hedge, then Satan would have seen it and wouldn't have had to ask God about it. Job let the hedge down when he walked in fear instead of faith. Job was fearful about his children that he continually made sacrifices for them.

> *"Then the Lord said to Satan, "Behold, all that he has is in your power, only do not put forth your hand on him." So Satan departed from the presence of the Lord." Job 1:12 New American Standard Bible*

God never said that He put everything into Satan's hands. God is stating a fact here that because of the fear Job was walking in (see Job 3:25) that Job had given legal right to Satan and Satan knew that. Job, because of fear, placed everything into Satan's hands.

> *"He said, "Naked I came from my mother's womb, And naked I shall return there.*

The Lord gave and the Lord has taken away. Blessed
be the name of the Lord." Job 1:21 New American
Standard Bible

Too many have misquoted Job. For some people, if their theology doesn't line up with their circumstances, then they twist scripture to fit their circumstances. That's not correct in God's eyes at all. I have heard so many quote "the Lord gives and the Lord takes away" at a child's funeral. God never said that. Job said it and if you read further and take the whole counsel of God, Job got corrected for saying that. John 10:10 says that the thief comes to steal, kill and destroy. Do you think God is a thief? Certainly not! We have to remember that Job said that statement of "the Lord gives and the Lord takes away" and not God. God later says that Job had "such ignorant words."

> *"Then the Lord answered Job out of the whirlwind,*
> *and said, Who is this that darkeneth counsel*
> *by words without knowledge?" Job 38:1-2 King*
> *James Version*

Why is God given credit for someone having cancer or "taking someone home early" when the Bible says *"I am the Lord that healeth thee."* God is not double-minded, nor does He have multiple personality disorder.

> *"The thief cometh not, but for to steal, and to kill,*
> *and to destroy: I am come that they might have life,*
> *and that they might have it more abundantly." John*
> *10:10 King James Version*

Illness isn't having an enjoyable life. People sometimes know that God can heal, but they wonder if God will heal. That's an insult to His character. He is the restorer of health, not the taker of health. He doesn't give it and then take it away.

"For I will restore health unto thee, and I will heal thee of thy wounds, saith the Lord; because they called thee an Outcast, saying, This is Zion, whom no man seeketh after." Jeremiah 30:17 King James Version

"But unto you that fear my name shall the Sun of righteousness arise with healing in his wings; and ye shall go forth, and grow up as calves of the stall." Malachi 4:2 King James Version

"And Jesus went about all Galilee, teaching in their synagogues, and preaching the gospel of the kingdom, and healing all manner of sickness and all manner of disease among the people. And his fame went throughout all Syria: and they brought unto him all sick people that were taken with divers diseases and torments, and those which were possessed with devils, and those which were lunatic, and those that had the palsy; and he healed them." Matthew 4:23-24 King James Version

Jesus is the same yesterday, today, and forever. He is the same healer today. We are also told in the Bible that we can do greater works (John 14:12) which includes miraculous healing.

"After this manner therefore pray ye: Our Father which art in heaven, Hallowed be thy name. Thy kingdom come, Thy will be done in earth, as it is in heaven." Matthew 6:9-10 King James Version

This verse is a good one for those that say, "They received their healing when they went home to be with the Lord. They don't have their illness in Heaven." I agree that there is no sickness in Heaven. However, God told us to pray that it would be that same way on earth like it is in Heaven! He wants the divine health that is in Heaven to be also on the Earth! There is also prosperity and worship in Heaven. God uses gold for pavement. He is not broke. No angel has a broken wing.

> *"The light of the body is the eye: if therefore thine eye be single, thy whole body shall be full of light. But if thine eye be evil, thy whole body shall be full of darkness. If therefore the light that is in thee be darkness, how great is that darkness!" Matthew 6:22-23 King James Version*

Be single in your focus. Your eyes can only see one direction at a time. You can either focus on the promises of God, or focus on the sickness in your body. If your eyes are singularly focused on the Word of God, the outcome will be healing and light as the scripture we just read states.

> *" And, behold, there came a leper and worshipped him, saying, Lord, if thou wilt, thou canst make me clean. And Jesus put forth his hand, and touched him, saying, I will; be thou clean. And immediately his leprosy was cleansed." Matthew 8:2-3 King James Version*

Jesus still says, "I will." His nature and character has not changed. You do not have to wonder what His will is. Receive His healing and enjoy your "immediately" miracle also!

> *"And when Jesus was entered into Capernaum, there came unto him a centurion, beseeching him, And saying, Lord, my servant lieth at home sick of the palsy, grievously tormented. And Jesus saith unto him, I will come and heal him." Matthew 8:5-7 King James Version*

Expect a miracle. Ask Him for a miracle. Do not waver which is to be double-minded while waiting for your miracle to manifest.

> *"When Jesus came into Peter's house, he saw Peter's mother-in-law lying in bed with a fever. He touched her hand and the fever left her, and she got up and began to wait on him. When evening came, many who were demon-possessed were brought to him, and he drove out the spirits with a word and healed all the sick. This was to fulfill what was spoken through the prophet Isaiah: "He took up our infirmities and bore our diseases." Matthew 8:14-17 New International Version*

It does not say that Jesus healed some, but that Jesus healed all (King James Version). He healed the sick! It never says that He let some stay ill because they were learning something! The sick and demon-possessed should be running to believers to be healed and delivered. Perhaps they do not come because we do not have the reputation of healing and delivering?!

> *"And, behold, a woman, which was diseased with an issue of blood twelve years, came behind him, and touched the hem of his garment: For she said within herself, If I may but touch his garment, I shall be whole. But Jesus turned him about, and when he saw her, he said, Daughter, be of good comfort; thy faith hath made thee whole. And the woman was made whole from that hour." Matthew 9:20-22 King James Version*

There you have another report of faith causing an instant miracle. Again I must remind you that I am simply quoting the Bible. All these scriptures are also in your Bible. This is not anything I am making up! Her faith in the healing power of Jesus

---

caused her to press in through the crowds in order to get to Jesus. As soon as she reached out to receive her miracle, she was healed. He is no respecter of persons (meaning that He does not look at your status or income). He is a respecter of faith. His love is unconditional, but His promises have conditions.

> *"And Jesus went about all the cities and villages, teaching in their synagogues, and preaching the gospel of the kingdom, and healing every sickness and every disease among the people." Matthew 9:35 King James Version*

Jesus went around healing every sickness and every disease. We are His disciples (His followers and His students)! We are Christians (which means little anointed ones). We are to be in this world doing as He was doing. After all, that is what He commissioned us to do.

> *"Herein is our love made perfect, that we may have boldness in the day of judgment: because as He is, so are we in this world."*
>
> *1 John 4:17 King James Version*
>
> *"Then He said to the man, "Stretch out your hand!" He stretched it out, and it was restored to normal, like the other." Matthew 12:13 New American Standard Bible*
>
> *"When He went ashore, He saw a large crowd, and felt compassion for them and healed their sick." Matthew 14:14 New American Standard Bible*
>
> *"And those who were in the boat worshiped Him, saying, "You are certainly God's Son!" When they had crossed over, they came to land at Gennesaret.*

And when the men of that place recognized Him,
they sent word into all that surrounding district
and brought to Him all who were sick; and they
implored Him that they might just touch the fringe
of His cloak; and as many as touched it were cured."
Matthew 14:33-36

Let the reputation spread about you and your church so that people bring all their sick to get healed.

In the book of Matthew, chapter 15, starting in verse 19 is where Jesus returned to the Sea of Galilee. A vast crowd brought to Him the lame, and others with various physical ailments. He healed them all. The crowd was amazed. The mute were now talking, the crippled were well, the lame were able to walk, and those who were blind could see! And they all praised God.

There you have yet another verse that says, "Jesus healed them all." I presented to you another verse that does not say that Jesus thought they needed to learn some more from their illness so He made them stay sick a while longer.

CHAPTER 16: MOUNTAIN MOVING FAITH

"And Jesus said unto them, Because of your unbelief: for verily I say unto you, If ye have faith as a grain of mustard seed, ye shall say unto this mountain, Remove hence to yonder place; and it shall remove; and nothing shall be impossible unto you."
Matthew 17:20 King James Version

God says that FAITH makes mountains move and makes all things possible. Don't get mad at me. I didn't write this Bible. I am just telling you what The Word of God says. The Bible is full of encouragement to develop and use our faith.

"And as they departed from Jericho, a great multitude followed him. And, behold, two blind men sitting by the way side, when they heard that Jesus passed by, cried out, saying, Have mercy on us, O Lord, thou son of David. And the multitude rebuked them, because they should hold their peace: but they cried the more, saying, Have mercy on us, O Lord, thou son of David. And Jesus stood still, and called them, and said, What will ye that I shall do unto you?

They say unto him, Lord, that our eyes may be opened.

So Jesus had compassion on them, and touched their eyes: and immediately their eyes received sight, and they followed him." Matthew 20:29-35 King James Version

Tell everyone that you are well, strong, and healed because you are "calling things that be not as if they were" (Romans 4:17). Calling things requires an action on your part involving your mouth. Remember that in Genesis, God created the heaven and earth by speaking. He spoke and things were created. As I have mentioned previously we are created in His image, so our words also have creative power.

"And Jesus answered and said to them, "Truly I say to you, if you have faith and do not doubt, you will not only do what was done to the fig tree, but even if you say to this mountain, 'Be taken up and cast into the sea,' it will happen." Matthew 21:21 New American Standard Bible

Matthew 21:21 Then Jesus told them, "I assure you, if you have faith and do not doubt, you can do all things like this and so much more." New Living Translation.

He is expecting us to do miracles and even greater works than He did. We have a job to do and in order to do it we need to start believing not doubting what the Word says. Remember, your theology can not be based on past experiences nor current circumstances. Theology must be based on the Word of God alone.

"Some people are like seed along the path, where the word is sown. As soon as they hear it, Satan comes

and takes away the word that was sown in them."
Mark 4:15 New International Version

Satan comes to steal away revelation of the Word regarding healing. You will have to stand in faith to apply every word of revelation knowledge you receive.

> *"While Jesus was still speaking, some people came from the house of Jairus, the synagogue leader. "Your daughter is dead," they said. "Why bother the teacher anymore?" Overhearing what they said, Jesus told him, "Don't be afraid; just believe." He did not let anyone follow him except Peter, James and John the brother of James." Mark 5:35-37 New International Version*

Jesus ignored their comments and said to Jairus, "Don't be afraid. Just trust Me." Jesus stopped the crowd and would not let anyone go with Him except Peter, James, and John.

Messengers will come to you with reports that you will have to ignore. Just as Jesus and Jairus ignored the bad report, so do we. Jesus looked straight at Jairus and instructed Jairus to trust Him. Jesus says the same thing to us. Watch who you let into your birthing room when you are birthing a miracle. Watch who speaks into your life as there will be some reports from people that you need to ignore. Jesus wouldn't let the unbelieving crowd into the room when He raised Jairus' daughter.

> *And he could there do no mighty work, save that he laid his hands upon a few sick folk, and healed them. And he marvelled because of their unbelief. And he went round about the villages, teaching"*
> *Mark 6:5-6 King James Version*

He was amazed at their unbelief. Is He amazed at your unbelief? It doesn't say that Jesus *wouldn't* do any miracles, but that He *couldn't*. Create the atmosphere for miracles.

> *"As soon as they got out of the boat, people recognized Jesus. 55 They ran throughout that whole region and carried the sick on mats to wherever they heard he was. 56 And wherever he went— into villages, towns or countryside—they placed the sick in the marketplaces. They begged him to let them touch even the edge of his cloak, and all who touched it were healed." Mark 6:54-56 New International Version*

> *And Jesus answered saying to them, "Have faith in God. 23 Truly I say to you, whoever says to this mountain, 'Be taken up and cast into the sea,' and does not doubt in his heart, but believes that what he says is going to happen, it will be granted him. 24 Therefore I say to you, all things for which you pray and ask, believe that you have received them, and they will be granted you." Mark 11:22-24 New American Standard Bible*

We need to act like the miracle has already been received and talk like it has already been received. Your flesh wants to see the manifestation first before it believes, but the spirit realm does not work that way. You will have what your mouth says that you are believing for.

> *And these signs shall follow them that believe; In my name shall they cast out devils; they shall speak with new tongues. They shall take up serpents; and if they drink any deadly thing, it shall not hurt them; they*

shall lay hands on the sick, and they shall recover."
Mark 16:17-18 King James Version

These signs followed believers around. They don't follow doubters or double-minded people around! If these signs are not accompanying us, I wonder if we need to check our belief level?!

> *"While the sun was setting, all those who had any who were sick with various diseases brought them to Him; and laying His hands on each one of them, He was healing them." Luke 4:40 New American Standard Bible*

> *"And he withdrew himself into the wilderness, and prayed. And it came to pass on a certain day, as he was teaching, that there were Pharisees and doctors of the law sitting by, which were come out of every town of Galilee, and Judaea, and Jerusalem: and the power of the Lord was present to heal them. And, behold, men brought in a bed a man which was taken with a palsy: and they sought means to bring him in, and to lay him before him. And when they could not find by what way they might bring him in because of the multitude, they went upon the housetop, and let him down through the tiling with his couch into the midst before Jesus. And when he saw their faith, he said unto him, Man, thy sins are forgiven thee." Luke 5:16-20 King James Version*

Again, faith is mentioned! Let us be this type of friend to people! Be the person who is willing to rip off a roof with bare hands to get people saved, healed, delivered, or raised from the dead. The four crazy friends probably later repaired the roof or paid for it to be repaired. Do whatever it takes to get people to Jesus!

"And he came down with them, and stood in the plain, and the company of his disciples, and a great multitude of people out of all Judaea and Jerusalem, and from the sea coast of Tyre and Sidon, which came to hear him, and to be healed of their diseases;And they that were vexed with unclean spirits: and they were healed.And the whole multitude sought to touch him: for there went virtue out of him, and healed them all." Luke 6:17-19 King James Version

He healed them all. "All" means everyone.

"And it came to pass the day after, that he went into a city called Nain; and many of his disciples went with him, and much people. Now when he came nigh to the gate of the city, behold, there was a dead man carried out, the only son of his mother, and she was a widow: and much people of the city was with her. And when the Lord saw her, he had compassion on her, and said unto her, Weep not. And he came and touched the bier: and they that bare him stood still. And he said, Young man, I say unto thee, Arise. And he that was dead sat up, and began to speak. And he delivered him to his mother. And there came a fear on all: and they glorified God, saying, That a great prophet is risen up among us; and, That God hath visited his people. And this rumour of him went forth throughout all Judaea, and throughout all the region round about." Luke 7:11-17 King James Version

What report is spreading about you? What report is being spread about the church? Are people seeing an alive, healing God when they see us, His followers? Our God is not dead! Our God is not deaf! He hears us and is alive in us with resurrection power! Every time Jesus went to a funeral He raised the person!

> " Then he called his twelve disciples together, and gave them power and authority over all devils, and to cure diseases. And he sent them to preach the kingdom of God, and to heal the sick." Luke 9:1-2 King James Version

> "And they departed, and went through the towns, preaching the gospel, and healing every where." Luke 9:6 King James Version

What impact are we making? Are we to sit in a pew at church and then back home never to reach to the world around us? We are also His disciples and have the same impact as the original twelve disciples.

> "And into whatsoever city ye enter, and they receive you, eat such things as are set before you: And heal the sick that are therein, and say unto them, The kingdom of God is come nigh unto you." Luke 10:8 King James Version

We are to go into towns and heal their sick. The kingdom of God is with us!!

> "And he was teaching in one of the synagogues on the sabbath. And, behold, there was a woman which had a spirit of infirmity eighteen years, and was bowed together, and could in no wise lift up herself. And when Jesus saw her, he called her to him, and said unto her, Woman, thou art loosed from thine infirmity. And he laid his hands on her: and immediately she was made straight, and glorified God." Luke 13:10-13 King James Version

God doesn't get any glory from sickness. When unbelievers get healed, they start praising God and become believers. If we thought that sickness and disease were from God and God's will, then we better condemn every doctor and nurse for trying to thwart God's will.

> *"And a certain man was there, which had an infirmity thirty and eight years. When Jesus saw him lie, and knew that he had been now a long time in that case, he saith unto him, Wilt thou be made whole? The impotent man answered him, Sir, I have no man, when the water is troubled, to put me into the pool: but while I am coming, another steppeth down before me. Jesus saith unto him, Rise, take up thy bed, and walk. And immediately the man was made whole, and took up his bed, and walked: and on the same day was the sabbath." John 5:5-9 King James Version*

> *"It is the Spirit that quickeneth (or makes alive); the flesh profits nothing: the words that I speak unto you, they are spirit and they are LIFE." John 6:63 King James Version*

The Word of God is more than just information. Every time you take the Word into your heart, believe it and act on it. Then that very life of God Himself that Jesus spoke of is released in you.

> *"Truly, truly, I say to you, he who believes in Me, the works that I do, he will do also; and greater works than these he will do; because I go to the Father. Whatever you ask in My name, that will I do, so that the Father may be glorified in the Son. If you ask Me anything in My name, I will do it." John 14:12-14 New American Standard Bible*

Jesus raised the dead and we are to do greater works! We are given permission to ask in Jesus' name. We have not because we ask not. The Greek work for ask in John 14:12-14 means "demand." It is not actually a prayer. In the book of Acts, the apostles didn't pray for the sick. They demanded in the name of Jesus that the sick rise up and walk.

> *"If you remain in me and my words remain in you, ask whatever you wish, and it will be done for you. 8 This is to my Father's glory, that you bear much fruit, showing yourselves to be my disciples." John 15:7-8 New International Version*

It doesn't say that we should bear little fruit or no fruit. Disciples are to bear much fruit. We are to be a sign and a wonder that is drawing people in. Crowds followed Jesus and the disciples to get healed and delivered. The crowds wanted to see miracles. He was okay with a miracle being what attracted them and, oh yes, He got them saved! Jesus didn't mind doing it that way.

> *" Now Peter and John went up together into the temple at the hour of prayer, being the ninth hour. And a certain man lame from his mother's womb was carried, whom they laid daily at the gate of the temple which is called Beautiful, to ask alms of them that entered into the temple; Who seeing Peter and John about to go into the temple asked an alms. And Peter, fastening his eyes upon him with John, said, Look on us. And he gave heed unto them, expecting to receive something of them. Then Peter said, Silver and gold have I none; but such as I have give I thee: In the name of Jesus Christ of Nazareth rise up and walk. And he took him by the right hand, and lifted him up: and immediately his feet and ankle bones received strength. And he leaping up*

stood, and walked, and entered with them into the temple, walking, and leaping, and praising God. And all the people saw him walking and praising God: And they knew that it was he which sat for alms at the Beautiful gate of the temple: and they were filled with wonder and amazement at that which had happened unto him. And as the lame man which was healed held Peter and John, all the people ran together unto them in the porch that is called Solomon's, greatly wondering." Acts 3:1-11 King James Version

This is how to have church: miracles, signs and wonders!

"At the hands of the apostles many signs and wonders were taking place among the people; and they were all with one accord in Solomon's portico. But none of the rest dared to associate with them; however, the people held them in high esteem. And all the more believers in the Lord, multitudes of men and women, were constantly added to their number, to such an extent that they even carried the sick out into the streets and laid them on cots and pallets, so that when Peter came by at least his shadow might fall on any one of them. Also the people from the cities in the vicinity of Jerusalem were coming together, bringing people who were sick or afflicted with unclean spirits, and they were all being healed." Acts 5:12-16 New American Standard Bible

We are His messengers on earth today, exhorted to heal the sick and deliver the oppressed. We are His ambassadors called to represent our home country of Heaven while here on earth. All were healed in Acts 5 and all could be healed now.

"Then Philip went down to the city of Samaria, and preached Christ unto them. And the people with one accord gave heed unto those things which Philip spake, hearing and seeing the miracles which he did. For unclean spirits, crying with loud voice, came out of many that were possessed with them: and many taken with palsies, and that were lame, were healed. And there was great joy in that city." Acts 8:5-8 King James Version

Philip did miracles and got people's attention. Our cities can use some great joy! People listened "intently" because the miracles got their ear. We need to be able to produce what we say we can produce.

"As Peter traveled about the country, he went to visit the Lord's people who lived in Lydda. There he found a man named Aeneas, who was paralyzed and had been bedridden for eight years. "Aeneas," Peter said to him, "Jesus Christ heals you. Get up and roll up your mat." Immediately Aeneas got up. All those who lived in Lydda and Sharon saw him and turned to the Lord." Acts 9:32-34 New International Version

The miracles happened and it changed the entire population of two towns. Let your whole town turn to the Lord because the lame got up and started walking around! We want our unsaved family, friends, neighbors and co-workers to be saved. We don't want people going to hell for all eternity. The whole population of Lydia and Sharon turned to the Lord because a miracle happened. In that verse, God is clearly telling us a powerful way to evangelize.

"How God anointed Jesus of Nazareth with the Holy Ghost and with power: who went about

doing good, and healing all that were oppressed of the devil; for God was with him." Acts 10:38 King James Version

If you are still asking God what you are supposed to be doing, you can get started by going around and doing good and healing all who are oppressed of the devil. God is with you and has anointed you. You don't need a word from God as to your ministry before you get off the couch. Just start by doing Acts 10:38. Start changing the entire town.

"At Lystra a man was sitting who had no strength in his feet, lame from his mother's womb, who had never walked. 9 This man was listening to Paul as he spoke, who, when he had fixed his gaze on him and had seen that he had faith to be made well, 10 said with a loud voice, "Stand upright on your feet." And he leaped up and began to walk." Acts 14: 8-10 New American Standard Bible

That is another verse that mentions faith. Paul spoke in a bold statement in a loud voice to the man in the wheelchair (to put it in today's vocabulary). He told the man to start walking and that is our mandate also!

"And God wrought special miracles by the hands of Paul: So that from his body were brought unto the sick handkerchiefs or aprons, and the diseases departed from them, and the evil spirits went out of them." Acts 19:11-12 King James Version

If we saw a preacher today putting a piece of cloth on someone (as Apostle Paul did there in Acts 19) and healings started taking place; would we criticize that person for being different or realize that it was God behind it?

"His father was sick in bed, suffering from fever and dysentery. Paul went in to see him and, after prayer, placed his hands on him and healed him. When this had happened, the rest of the sick on the island came and were cured. They honored us in many ways; and when we were ready to sail, they furnished us with the supplies we needed." Acts 28:8-10 New International Version

Paul went in and prayed for that man. Laying his hands on him, he healed him. Then, all the other sick people on the island came and were cured. As a result, people showered them with gifts. When the time came to sail, people put on board all sorts of things they would need for the trip.

"(As it is written, I have made thee a father of many nations,) before him whom he believed, even God, who quickeneth the dead, and calleth those things which be not as though they were." Romans 4:17 King James Version

The word "calleth" here in Romans 4:17 means "summons to appear", like in a court of law. When you call something into existence that wasn't there before (healing or finances or...) then a summons is released in the spirit realm and now it must appear in the natural. Start calling in the fulfillment of your dreams because only you can choose to either abort it or give birth to it. Abraham went around calling himself the father of many nations for years before he had any children in the natural.

"yet, with respect to the promise of God, he did not waver in unbelief but grew strong in faith, giving glory to God," Romans 4:20 New American Standard Bible

You need to stay in the word until you do not waver in unbelief.

"That if thou shalt confess with thy mouth the Lord Jesus, and shalt believe in thine heart that God hath raised him from the dead, thou shalt be saved. For with the heart man believeth unto righteousness; and with the mouth confession is made unto salvation." Romans 10:9-10 King James Version

The mouth and heart are two places that faith must be for results to manifest.

In Greek, the word salvation is *sozo* which literally means, "to be made sound, to be delivered from every form of danger, both temporal and eternal." Refuse to let Satan put any foul thing on your body after Jesus already carried it for you. You have to stand and fight the good fight of faith.

"Casting down imaginations, and every high thing that exalteth itself against the knowledge of God, and bringing into captivity every thought to the obedience of Christ" 2 Corinthians 10:5 King James Version

"So again I ask, does God give you his Spirit and work miracles among you by the works of the law, or by your believing what you heard?" Galatians 3:5 New International Version

"For the Word that God speaks is alive and full of power [making it active, operative, energizing, and effective]; it is sharper than any two-edged sword, penetrating to the dividing line of the breath of life (soul) and [the immortal] spirit, and of joints and marrow [of the deepest parts of our nature], exposing and sifting and analyzing and judging the very thoughts and purposes of the heart." Hebrews 4:12 Amplified Bible

Scripture is alive and full of power. Every time you take in a dose of the Word of God, it effects your mind and affects your body as well as your spirit.

In Hebrews chapter 6 from verses 16 to 20 speaks about taking a binding oath. God bound Himself with an oath, so that those who received the promise could know that they know that it is a binding agreement. So God has given us both His promise and His oath. These two things are completely unchangeable as it is impossible for God to lie.

Sarah Scarrow

The Witness Center

thewitnesscenter@gmail.com